ONLINE BUSINESS FROM SCRATCH

Launch Your Own Seven-Figure Internet Business by Creating and Selling Information Online

Praise for *Online Business from Scratch*

Matthew Paulson is the real deal. I've made millions using the same strategies that he outlines in *Online Business from Scratch*, and this guide will give new and experienced internet entrepreneurs alike a roadmap for success and profit. The best part is that this model is incredibly sustainable—this will work today, tomorrow, and for years to come—unlike most strategies that most people teach. Had I been given this roadmap when I started my career, I would have avoided years of struggle and lost revenue. This is a must read for anyone who has something to share and wants to get paid for it.

Ryan Daniel Moran,
Founder of Freedom Fastlane
www.freedomfastlane.com

If you dream of making a living online and escaping the nine-to-five, *Online Business from Scratch* will IGNITE your entrepreneurial journey by giving you a proven plan that actually works and by inspiring you to take massive action. Whether you're technologically illiterate or a geek, Online Business from Scratch can help turn your dream of owning an online business into reality.

John Lee Dumas,
Host of Entrepreneur On Fire
www.eofire.com

With so much noise and bad information in the world of online business, it's refreshing to see proven and actionable advice from an entrepreneur that has actually done it. *Online Business from Scratch* offers a proven plan that will guide anyone who is willing to learn and put in consistent effort to build their own Internet business.

Jaime Masters,
Eventual Millionaire
www.eventualmillionaire.com

An online business requires no lease, no employees, and no daily commute. Here's a guide to take those advantages and open the door to your own unlimited income and the time freedom to enjoy it.

Dan Miller,
Author and Coach
www.48days.com

Matthew Paulson is not just another internet marketing guru. He's a guy that actually has built multiple six-figure and seven-figure online businesses from the ground up and is constantly pushing the envelope with new marketing techniques and creative monetization strategies. If you really want to build and grow an online business, start with Matthew's content.

Andrew Warner,
Host of Mixergy
www.mixergy.com

A highly detailed blueprint for any beginner looking to start an online business, written by someone who's done it many times.

Rob Walling,
co-founder of Drip,
co-host of MicroConf and Startups for the Rest of Us

ONLINE BUSINESS FROM SCRATCH

Launch Your Own Seven-Figure Internet Business by Creating and Selling Information Online

MATTHEW PAULSON

Online Business from Scratch:
Launch Your Own Seven-Figure Internet Business by Creating and
Selling Information Online

Published by American Consumer News, LLC.
First edition: February 2017
ISBN: 978-1539737674

Cover design: Rebecca McKeever
Editing: Craft Your Content (CraftYourContent.com)
Book Design: James Woosley (FreeAgentPress.com)
Printing: Amazon CreateSpace

TABLE OF CONTENTS

INTRODUCTION

THE YEAR WAS 1996. I was in the fourth or fifth grade, and my parents had purchased a desktop computer as a Christmas present for our family. It was a Packard Bell that ran Windows 95, had a 14-inch screen, 16 megabytes of RAM, and a 133MHZ Pentium processor. They got dial-up internet access from a local ISP called SunriseNet, and we were able to use the internet for a whopping 20 hours per month using a 28.8Kb/sec dial-up modem.

My parents saw the computer as a way to create Word documents, look up information online, and play a few games, but I saw a world of opportunity. Even at 11 years old, I recognized that computers were going to play an increasingly important role in our everyday lives for years to come, and I was incredibly curious about what I could do with our home computer.

Like most other kids who had a computer, I used ours to play a lot of video games. My first love was SimCity 2000 and its many spin-offs, including SimTower, SimCopter, SimEarth, SimAnt and Streets of SimCity. I also played an early MMORPG (Massive Multiplayer Online Role-Playing Game) called Nexus-TK and a couple of strategy games, including Subspace and BattleCity.

My love for technology didn't end at playing computer games.

I also saw our family computer as a way to create things. I had always loved building things with blocks and Legos in my childhood. Creating things on the computer was the next logical step. Since the web was just coming into the mainstream, I took it upon myself to learn HTML and, using GeoCities, made a really bad homepage for myself that contained a bunch of animated gifs.

Sometime after I had built my personal website, I was searching for SimCity 2000 cheat codes, and I came across a number of fan-built websites that shared news, tips, tricks, saved-games, and cheat codes for some of my other favorite games. Since I knew some basic HTML, I figured I could also build a website for my favorite SimCity games, specifically. I pulled out my favorite HTML editor at the time, DiDaPro, and began working on creating my very own SimCity fan website.

I worked on the website after school and on weekends for a few weeks, and soon enough the first iteration of my SimCity fan website, *SimWeb*, was born. It had screenshots, cheat codes, utilities, tips, tricks, and saved games for all of my favorite SimCity games. It was hosted by a company called Xoom.com. I even put a hit counter on my website to see how many people were visiting it. I didn't do any marketing beyond submitting it to a bunch of search engines and somehow, after about six months, around 25 people were visiting my website daily.

I then heard that you could make money from a website

by putting ads on it, so I signed up for a now-defunct affiliate network, called SafeAudit, and put up ads promoting free web hosting accounts. After a couple of months, enough people had clicked through the ads and signed up for free web hosting accounts of their own, that I reached the minimum threshold to receive my first payment.

I will never forget the day that my dad told me, "Matthew, you received a check in the mail today for $30.00. What do you want me to do with it?" Though I was only 12 years old, I had realized that you really could make money on the internet.

For the remainder of my middle school years, I ran my little SimCity fan website and netted around $25.00 per month from it. That might not seem like a lot of money to most people, but when I was 12 years old and getting a $1.00 per week allowance, having $25.00 in my pocket made me feel like a millionaire. When I entered high school, the affiliate network I was part of shut down, and I stopped making money.

My first online business venture was over, but at least I knew that it was possible to make money online, if you were willing to put in the work.

From SimWeb to MarketBeat

It wasn't until my junior year of college that I started my second online business venture: a personal finance blog called American Consumer News. I won't dive into that story in great detail, because I've already shared it at length in my other books. American Consumer News eventually evolved into my current online business, MarketBeat, which offers stock research tools and publishes a popular investment newsletter with more than 450,000 active subscribers. MarketBeat generated $2.7 million in revenue last year, attracted more than 40 million pageviews, and was named one of the 5,000 fastest-growing, privately-held companies in the United States by Inc. Magazine in 2016.

I have launched a number of other online businesses, some of which have failed miserably and others that have done well. I launched a community website for audiobook listeners that went nowhere. I launched a press release service that generated five figures in monthly revenue, but I hated running it, so I sold it off. I tried to create a podcast management and listening service (think Stitcher) that never got off the ground. I assisted in creating GoGo Photo Contest, which has helped animal shelters raise more than $3 million over the course of two and a half years. I also own a piece of USGolfTV—a digital publishing company that sells instructional products to the golf industry.

While I've had some success in the online business world, I don't tell you all of these things to brag or put myself up on a pedestal. The only reason I've included a couple of paragraphs about the success I've had is so you can be sure you're reading a book by someone that has actually done it several times over. This is important.

There are far too many books that promise to teach you to "make money online" or generate "passive income" which are written by people who have never actually done it themselves or who have only ever made money online by teaching other people to make money online.

As you read the strategies and best practices I outline in this book, you can rest assured that they are grounded in experience and actually work, because I've tested them out in my own successful online businesses.

Why Write Another Book?

In early 2014, I published my first nonfiction book, which was titled *40 Rules for Internet Business Success* (www.40rulesbook.com). The purpose of the book was to teach the principles and strategies that I have used to build my online businesses. More than 10,000 copies of *40 Rules for Internet*

Business Success have been sold, and many people wrote me to tell me they were inspired to start their own internet business as a result.

The book was a success in its own right and offers great insight into how I think about building businesses, but it was never designed to be a comprehensive guide for anyone looking to launch their own online business. You can learn a lot of great principles to apply in your business by reading *40 Rules for Internet Business Success*, but you wouldn't be able to read the book and know exactly where to start to launch your own online business.

In 2015, I published *Email Marketing Demystified* (www.myemailmarketingbook.com), a book which teaches the email marketing strategies I use at MarketBeat, GoGo Photo Contest, and USGolfTV. I published *The Ten-Year Turnaround* (www.tenyearturnaround.com) in 2016, which teaches readers how they can achieve financial freedom in ten years or less. I also published a collection of short-form business articles I've written in a book called *Business Growth Day by Day* (www.businessgrowthdaybyday.com) in 2016.

Though these books presented a lot of the business lessons I'd learned over the years, I realized I had never unpacked my pathway to success in a detailed fashion.

For this book, I decided to return to my core competency of launching and growing online businesses, and create a step-by-step guide that anyone can follow to build their own. I wanted to create a book that was accessible to people that don't have a strong technical background so that literally anyone with basic computer skills could launch their own online business. I also wanted the book to be comprehensive and cover every topic that an entrepreneur would need to know to grow their business to seven figures in annual revenue.

I began outlining and writing in mid-2016, and the fruit of

that labor is the book you are reading now: *Online Business from Scratch.*

Your Online Success Story Begins Here

You may already know the names of several normal people that have successfully launched online businesses, such as Jaime Masters, Jason Van Orden, John Lee Dumas, Jeff Walker, Pat Flynn, or Ryan Moran. You may have read their books or actively listen to their podcasts.

What you may not know is that for every one well-known online business expert, there are at least 20 more online entrepreneurs that make just as much money (if not more) that don't put their names out there, write books, and launch podcasts.

These online entrepreneurs all across the world don't broadcast their success, and quietly earn more than $100,000 per year in annual income. I'm talking about people like Abdul S. Mohammed (www.startabusinessforcheap.com) who makes money online by selling stuff on Etsy and by teaching people to follow their passion on YouTube. There's also Stephanie Palmer (www.goodinaroom.com), who teaches screenwriters to write better screenplays, Chuck Mullins, who runs a website that helps people follow the paleo diet (www.paleoplan.com) and Ruchi Vasishta, who makes mobile apps and sells physical products on Amazon. Given some time, I could probably come up with the names of at least 100 more online entrepreneurs that are making six figures in annual revenue that you've never heard of.

The people that I mentioned weren't born with a silver spoon in their mouths. They don't hold prestigious degrees, haven't received venture funding from Silicon Valley, and weren't apprentices to multi-millionaire entrepreneurs. They are normal people like you that decided to take action, work hard, and launch their own online businesses.

I'm not saying that launching a profitable online business is easy, but if you're willing to learn a lot and work hard, you too can build a profitable internet business.

The Authority Publishing Model

There are many different models that you can follow to build an online business. You can import physical products from China and sell them on Amazon or on your own ecommerce store. You can become an affiliate marketer and earn money promoting other people's products and services. You can create a software-as-a-service product and charge a recurring monthly fee for it. You can build mobile apps and publish them to Apple's App Store or the Google Play Store. You can create crafts and sell them on Etsy, or write books and publish them on Amazon.

There are many valid business models that afford people the opportunity to make money online, but my favorite online business model involves creating content for a specific niche, building an audience, and generating revenue through online advertising and by selling digital products. This business model is referred to as the **authority publishing business model**, because it involves becoming *an expert authority* on a specific subject, and publishing content around that subject.

The idea is that you serve the natural audience that is already interested in your subject, or niche, by creating content specifically targeted to them. You also create digital products, such as online courses and ebooks, for your audience to buy; and you can generate additional revenue by placing ads relevant to your niche on your website as well.

You might hear the phrase "authority publishing business" and assume that this business involves writing and publishing actual books. This usually isn't the case. A small percentage of online entrepreneurs write books to help promote their authority publishing business, but most don't. Instead, they focus on short-form content that's easier to produce and easier to consume, such as articles, social media posts, and online courses.

I use the authority publishing business model for Market-Beat. We publish financial news and information on our website in order to attract an audience, build our email list, and generate revenue from display advertising. Once our readers sign up for our email list, they receive our free daily newsletter that contains offers for our premium subscription products, that range from $14.97 per month to $34.97 per month.

We also generate revenue from our email list by including cost-per-click ads in our newsletter and periodically sending dedicated emails to our list on behalf of advertisers. This business model has served our company extremely well throughout the years, allowing us to grow revenue 729 percent between 2012 and 2015, while maintaining a profit margin of greater than 80 percent.

There are a lot of things to like about the authority publishing model.

The Pros of the Authority Publishing Model

Here are some reasons that you might choose to start an authority publishing business over some of the other online business models I mentioned earlier in the chapter:

- **Minimal Operating Expenses** – It doesn't cost a lot of money to launch an authority publishing business model. In my first full year of running an online business, my company generated $12,600 in revenue and had expenses that totaled a whopping $461.63. There are no inventory costs, and most of the strategies that you will use to build your audience won't cost you any money. You'll have to pay for a domain name, a hosting account, an email service provider, and maybe a few dollars to contractors here and there; but otherwise, there aren't a lot of expenses required to run an authority publishing business.

- **High Margins** – Since authority publishing businesses have minimal operating expenses, you get to keep almost all the money that you bring in. When you sell physical products through an ecommerce store, you will be lucky to keep 30 to 40 percent of your gross revenue. In authority publishing business models, generating a profit margin of 80 percent or more is very common.

- **High Scalability** – The amount of work you have to do to maintain the operations of your online business won't be that different if you generate $100,000 or $1,000,000 per year in revenue. You only have to create a piece of content once, regardless of how many people read it. You can also create a digital product once, and sell it over and over again to different people. You might need more help with customer support and a beefier web hosting account, but other than that, there's not substantially more work for you to do as your business grows.

- **Minimal Risk** – If your authority publishing business doesn't work out, you can always just cancel your web hosting account, shut down your website, and move on to your next project. Your authority publishing business probably won't have any long-term contracts to unwind, physical property to dispose of, or complicated legal setups that you have to undo. There's just not a lot that can come back to haunt you after your business has shut down (unless you fail to pay your taxes).

- **Passive Income** – Don't get me wrong here. I'm not saying that you can do work once and generate revenue forever; however, your ongoing revenue isn't directly tied to you working on your business regularly. This means that you can take a vacation for a couple weeks here and there and still generate revenue while you're not working.

The Cons of the Authorlty Publishing Model

Of course, there are downsides with every business model too. Here are some drawbacks of following the authority publishing model that this book teaches:

- **No Guarantee of Success** – You might choose a niche, pick a brand, build a website, create content, and try to market it for six months only to find out that you're not getting any traction and your online business isn't going to work out. You might seemingly be doing everything right, and still not achieve the success that you want. The strategies in Chapter 1 will help you avoid picking a bad niche and help you choose a niche that's likely to succeed, but there are no guarantees that your online business will take off.

- **Significant Time Commitment** – You have a lot of different balls to juggle when running an online business. You have to maintain your website, create content, promote your content, run your social media channels, manage your ad placements, and create digital products. In order to do all of these tasks well, you will need to invest a significant amount of time into your online business, at least in the beginning. If you are starting your authority publishing business on the side, expect to be putting at least 15 hours per week into your business on nights and weekends for the first two years.

- **Niches Change Over Time** – You might choose a niche that is popular when you launch your online business, only to find out a year or two later that the niche you selected was largely a fad. If you had launched a blog about the television show *Lost* in 2005, you would have done quite well until the show ended in 2010. When the *Lost* series ended, you would probably have seen a dramatic decline in traffic, as *Lost* fans moved on to other TV shows. To avoid this problem, try to choose a niche that has been around for awhile, has some staying power, and does not have an expected end date (so, not a book series, television show, one-time sporting event, etc.).

- **Dependent on Large Companies** – Most of your traffic will likely come via large companies whose interests aren't necessarily aligned with yours, like Google, Facebook, Twitter, and Apple. You might find a marketing strategy that works very well using one of these platforms, only to have them change an algorithm or change how they refer traffic to websites. You could lose a significant portion of your website traffic overnight, and would have no recourse to fix the problem. For this reason, it's very important to diversify your traffic sources and build an email list so that you can communicate with your audience, whether or not a big company continues to send you web traffic.

While there are some downsides to building an authority publishing business, I still believe the benefits of basing your business on the authority publishing model far outweigh any negative aspects.

Your Audience Is Your Business

The most important concept to understand about the authority publishing business model is that your audience truly is your business. In order for your business to work, you need an audience of people that regularly visits your websites, follows your social media accounts, buys your digital products, and clicks on the ads on your website.

Without these things, you don't have a business. You only have unloved social media accounts and a website that nobody visits. You absolutely must attract a group of followers that are passionate about your niche and love your content in order for your business to succeed.

Given this reality, it's important to create content that people actually want to read. Additionally, you will need to spend a significant amount of time marketing your website, the content that you produce, and your social media accounts.

The size of your audience will be the only factor that limits your business's growth. If you want to grow your business and generate more revenue, you will need to grow the size of your audience so that more people buy your digital products and click on the ads on your website. The way to do this is to produce helpful and engaging content that people in your niche enjoy reading, and by marketing your website through your social media accounts and other marketing channels.

Marketing is 50 Percent of The Work

Twenty years ago, when Yahoo was all the rage, you could build a website about a certain topic, and people would come just because it was a new website on the internet. The mantra of "build it and they will come" actually worked in the mid-'90s, but it doesn't any more.

Google has now indexed more than 30 trillion distinct web pages in its search engine—that's 30,000,000,000,000. Building a website offers no guarantee that anyone will ever actually come. Your website is effectively a brochure for your business, and brochures don't do any good if you leave them in your office and never hand them out to anyone.

For your online business to work, you must actively market your website as you would any other business. In fact, marketing an online business takes just as much time and effort as it does to actually build the website and create the content.

For every one hour you spend working on your website or creating, you should spend another hour marketing your business by publishing content on social media, doing guest blog posts on other websites, getting yourself booked as a guest on other people's podcasts, implementing paid advertising strategies, and testing other marketing techniques.

The Hub and Spoke Model

Using the authority publishing business model, your website will serve as the hub for all of your online business activities. Your other marketing channels will serve as spokes that drive people back to your website.

You will post all of your content to your website, place ads on your website, and sell your digital products on your website. If someone wants to learn more about your business, the best place for them to go should be your website.

You will also leverage a variety of other publishing channels in your business, like Facebook, Pinterest, Twitter, and YouTube. Social media channels should primarily be "spokes" that drive people back to the hub of your online business—your website. It's dangerous to let social media accounts become separate hubs of their own, because you don't own your Facebook Page, your Twitter account, or YouTube channel.

If you rub someone the wrong way or your account is on the wrong side of a platform change, your big social media following could be taken away from you, or become a lot less valuable, in an instant. That's why the primary focus of using social media should always be to send people back to your website so that they can read your content, sign-up for your email list, buy your digital products and click on your ads. You have 100 percent control over what happens on your website, unlike your social media profiles, which makes it the perfect home for your online presence.

The Power of Email in Online Business

Your email list will be the single most important asset in your online business. It will provide you a channel to directly communicate with your audience on a day-to-day basis, without forcing them to return to your website.

Your email list will become the primary sales channel for your digital products and may even become its own significant source of revenue for your business. You can use your email list to let your readers know about new content that you have produced, get feedback from your audience, communicate with your audience on a more personal level, promote your digital products, and generate affiliate commissions by selling other people's products.

Your email list will be far more valuable than a Twitter following, Facebook Fan Page, or audience you have built on any other social network. While you *can* build an audience using social networks like Instagram, Facebook, and Twitter, you don't own that audience and someone else can take it away from you without recourse at a moment's notice.

People that built Facebook Fan Pages early on learned this lesson the hard way. Fans of Facebook Pages used to receive almost 100 percent of the updates that pages posted, but then Facebook changed its algorithm so that less than 10 percent of a fan page's followers will see the page's updates. Page owners now have to pay to reach their entire audience.

Be wary of building an audience on someone else's platform whose business interests aren't aligned with yours. Since email is a federated standard that no single company owns and doesn't change very often, you will always have the ability to communicate with your audience through your email list.

When you're first getting started, email might seem like a small and inconsequential part of your business. You are probably not going to generate many digital product sales if you only have a few hundred followers, but remember that the size of your list is cumulative. Every month you'll add new subscribers, and before you know it you'll have several thousand. As time passes and your list grows, email will become an increasingly important communication and revenue generation tool for your business.

The key is to get started right away and put opt-in forms on your website from day one.

The sooner that you start collecting email addresses and sending emails to your audience, the sooner you will be able to receive a positive return on investment (ROI) from the effort you put into building your list.

It's Not Easy

There is a lot of misinformation and hype in the online business training space, especially from people that teach others how to build online businesses. Many "online business experts" have only ever made money online by teaching other people how to make money online.

Self-proclaimed gurus show off pictures of themselves in mansions, expensive cars, and high-end yachts that they claim to have purchased using the money from their online business. In reality, the mansions, expensive cars and yachts are short-term rentals that they used to give the appearance of wealth where none actually exists.

Some people claim that you can make $10,000 a month just by working a few hours per week—usually these are the same people trying to sell you an expensive online course or private coaching that can cost several thousand dollars. Unfortunately, the mythical four-hour work week doesn't actually exist.

If you think you're going to throw up a website and be making thousands of dollars a month after a few months, don't bother trying to build an online business. You are only going to end up disappointed. You have to put in long hours over the course of several years in order to build a successful online business. It doesn't have to be your full-time job, but if you actually want to get your business off the ground, expect to put in between 15 and 20 hours per week on top of your full-time job for at least a year before you get any meaningful traction.

I put about 20 hours per week into my online business when I was first getting started in 2007. By the end of 2007, I was making around $1,000 per month from Google AdSense and some private ad deals I had at the time. It wasn't until three years later that my monthly revenue exceeded a run rate of $100,000 per year. It took another four years after that to reach a monthly run rate of $1,000,000 per year.

Building an authority publishing business is not a way to generate short-term cash. It's a long-term strategy that requires discipline, focus, and consistent work over the course of several years.

What You'll Learn in Online Business from Scratch

Online Business from Scratch is a comprehensive guide that anyone can follow to build their own authority publishing business. This book contains a total of nine chapters, each of which contains an important aspect of building an online business.

Here's an overview of what's covered in this book:

- **Chapter One: Selecting Your Niche** – This chapter will show you how to pick a niche that you are passionate about, but will also be profitable to pursue. You will learn how to pick a niche that has strong advertiser demand and a base of followers that are ready and willing to buy digital products from you.

- **Chapter Two: Choosing a Name For Your Business** – This chapter will help you identify the perfect name for your business. You'll also learn how to get a good domain name that's not already taken, and learn how to get a great logo made for your business.

- **Chapter Three: Launching Your Website** – This chapter covers the nuts and bolts of putting your website together. You'll learn about getting a web hosting account, setting up WordPress, putting a theme in place, setting up plugins, and everything that you need to do to launch your website.

- **Chapter Four: Content Strategy and Content Marketing** – This chapter will help you develop a system to consistently create great content for your website. You will learn what social media networks and other publishing platforms are right for your business. You'll also learn how to optimize the content of your website for search engines and how to come up with ideas so that writer's block is never an issue.

- **Chapter Five: Additional Marketing Strategies** – In this chapter, you will learn how to leverage the power of email marketing in your business. I'll cover how to effectively use guest posts and podcast tours to build your audience. You'll discover the power of paid advertising strategies and how to identify what marketing channels your competitors are using.

- **Chapter Six: Making Money with Advertising** – This chapter reveals the four different ways that you can make money from your online business. You'll learn how to generate revenue by putting display ads on your website and by promoting affiliate offers. You'll also learn how to find the best combination of ad networks to maximize your advertising revenue, and how to make money with your email list.

- **Chapter Seven: Making Money with Digital Products** – You'll learn the types of digital products that are commonly sold by authority publishing businesses and why people will want to buy digital products from you. You'll learn how to create your first digital product and how to make sure your digital product launch is a success.

- **Chapter Eight: Creating Systems and Building a Team** – In this chapter, I'll explain the importance of building a team to run your business and how to find and hire your first team members. You will also learn to effectively lead and manage your team and use systems and standard operating procedures to grow and scale your business.

- **Chapter Nine: Putting it All Together** – In the final chapter, you'll learn how to put all of these strategies together and develop a 21-day action plan to launch your online business.

A Call to Action

We live in a world where it's entirely possible to build a six-figure or seven-figure online business with your laptop. Thousands of other people just like you have already built profitable online businesses by using their existing knowledge base, learning the intricacies of selling online, and consistently working on their businesses over a long period of time.

Many have quit their day jobs to go full time with their online businesses and others have built healthy side businesses that they run on nights and weekends. Launching your own online business will take your best mental energy, a lot of grit, diligence, and endurance; but it can also be an incredibly profitable and rewarding experience.

In *40 Rules for Internet Business Success*, I closed the introduction by saying that the best time to launch your online business was five years ago, but the second best time to start your online business is today.

Think about where you would like to be five years from now.

Do you want to be working at the same job you are today, or do you want to be running your own profitable online business full time? Time will pass regardless of whether or not you take action. Make a decision today and start working to get your project off the ground. You will be able to look back five years from now and be thankful and satisfied that you put the time, energy, and hustle in to launch your own online business.

For a few years, you'll have to do the work that most people aren't willing to do to build your online business. After that, you will be able to spend the rest of your life doing things that other people can't do: setting your own hours, working where you want and when you want, not having to worry about money, and having the freedom to travel wherever you please.

If you follow the guidance in this book and are willing to do the work, you too could someday have your very own profitable online business, and a lifestyle of your choosing.

CHAPTER ONE

Selecting Your Niche

IF YOU PLAN ON starting your own authority publishing business, your first major task is to determine what subject matter you want to focus on. The segment of the market that you choose, known as your niche, will help define your brand, your messaging, the content you create, and the products you sell.

Everything that you do in your business should fall under the umbrella of the niche you select.

At MarketBeat, our niche is stock research. Our brand, our content, the advertisers we work with, the products we sell, and everything else we do is directly related to researching stock investments in one way or another. If we happen upon an idea that has nothing to do with researching stocks, we simply don't do it. Our audience expects quality stock research tools and investing information from us and nothing else.

USGolfTV's niche is golf instruction and news. On the US-GolfTV website, we only produce content that helps golfers play a better game or informs them about the latest happenings in golf. Our membership site (www.myvirtualgolfcoach.com) and our video courses are solely focused on helping people play better golf. On our television show and our YouTube channel, we exclusively create videos to help golfers improve their game.

Everything that we do falls under the umbrella of golf instruction and news. If we tried to cover basketball, baseball, and football as well, we would do a pretty poor job trying to be everything to everyone. By exclusively focusing on a single sport, we can serve our audience to create content and products that they love.

You might find that choosing your niche is a challenging process. It can be very difficult to select a single topic as the basis for a business that will preoccupy you for the next several years. You might have several ideas that you are considering. You might have one idea, but aren't sure whether or not it's the right idea to pursue.

You might think there are already too many established players in your market. You might feel like you're not yet qualified to become a content creator in the niche that interests you. You might be afraid of choosing the wrong idea and regretting your decision later.

The remainder of this chapter will help you cut through these fears and other hang-ups to help you select the single niche that will become the basis of your business.

In this chapter, you will learn:

- Why you should only start a business you are extremely passionate about.

- Why niching down too far will limit your business's upside potential.

- Why you should choose a market that already has existing competitors.

- How to find a market with customers that are ready and willing to buy products and services from you.

- How to find a market with strong advertiser demand.

- How to choose between multiple niche ideas.

Pick Your Passion

In 2015, I attended a conference for software entrepreneurs called Microconf (www.microconf.com). One of the speakers, Patrick McKenzie (www.kalzumeus.com), told the story of how he launched his online scheduling business, Appointment Reminder (www.appointmentreminder.org). Massage therapists, hair salons, healthcare facilities, and client services businesses are based entirely on taking appointments with customers. If the customer doesn't show up to the appointment, the business loses money.

McKenzie knew that if he created a piece of software to remind customers of their appointments, no-show rates would go down, and his clients would make more money. When McKenzie announced the business in 2010 (http://www.kalzumeus.com/2010/05/14/unveiling-my-second-product-demo-included), his pitch was based entirely on the business need for such a service and his ability to create software to address the market's need. He had nothing to say about his personal excitement or passion for his business.

During his 2015 Microconf presentation, McKenzie said that "the most important piece of advice that I have ever ignored" was that you have to love what you do.

He recalled a conversation that he had with his friend Peldi Guilizzoni when he first launched his business. Guilizzoni asked him, "Will you really get up in the morning thinking, 'I will love if I spend today optimizing the schedules of dentist offices'?"

McKenzie responded, "God no! Of course not! Who would want that? But it's a great business. [Appointment Reminder] will clearly work well."

Guilizzoni replied, "Stop! Don't do it! You're going to spend the next five years of your life working on this thing. If you don't bounce up out of bed with excitement for it every morning, you're not going to do the work to push it forward and you're going to be miserable with yourself."

McKenzie said that choosing a business that he wasn't passionate about was the worst mistake he had made during the last ten years.

McKenzie closed by saying that one of the biggest unfair advantages that you can have in a business is product-market-founder fit. If you are working in an industry that you actually care about, are solving a problem that you actually care about, and you are the right person to build that product, you will have an incredible advantage over people that don't share your enthusiasm and interest.

You can view the entire video of McKenzie's Microconf presentation on Vimeo at https://vimeo.com/129913527.

Should you be successful, you will be operating your business for the next five to ten years. You are playing a long-term game. Choose a niche that excites you, that you can see yourself working on for a while. Don't choose a topic area because you feel like you can make a lot of money with it or because you feel like it would be an easy market to attack. You should only choose a niche because you are genuinely excited about the space and want to become a leading expert in it. While your personal passion shouldn't be the only criteria you use to select a niche, it should be at the top of the list.

Let Personal Experience Guide You

You should have some level of firsthand experience or interest in the niche you select. It will be much easier to create content, products, and services for a market that you already understand than one that you don't. If you are choosing a niche that you have no personal experience with or knowledge in, you will be facing an uphill battle. It means you will have to both learn the market you're entering, and then somehow create differentiated products and services that people in that market will want to buy. If you already know the market you're entering, you likely already know what the people in your market need, and what weaknesses there are with existing products and services in the space.

You will ideally be part of your own target market, and have experienced the needs and wants of the market firsthand, but that's not always possible. Your target market does not necessarily need to be other people who are exactly like you, but you should have a close relationship with someone in your target market. Maybe your mom, one of your siblings, a close personal friend, or a business acquaintance is part of the target market you are hoping to serve. By having someone close to you, you can bounce ideas off of them and get feedback about your content.

For example, GoGo Photo Contest (www.gogophotocontest.com) helps animal welfare groups raise money through online photo contest fundraisers. Neither I, nor the other two co-founders of the business, have ever worked at an animal shelter. However, we are incredibly passionate about the work that we do and are able to bounce ideas off the people at our local humane society, where one of our founders is a board member. While we don't have firsthand experience running an animal shelter, we are close enough to enough people in the market, so we understand and can effectively serve its needs.

Don't Niche Down Too Far

A common piece of advice given by internet business gurus is that you should "niche down until it hurts." The idea is that you should pick a small subsection of an existing market so you can serve that niche better than anyone else and become the go-to resource for your niche.

For instance, you might be interested in aquariums and having fish in your home, and decide to make this your target market. The "niche down until it hurts" ideology would suggest that you focus on a specific kind of fish, and only on the breeding or care of that specific type of fish. Instead of choosing "aquariums" as your niche, your niche might be "goldfish breeding".

In this case, the experts are wrong—especially if you want to build a large business.

When you "niche down until it hurts," you will often end up selecting a very small market, which will significantly limit your ability to build a large business over the long term. Even if you were to build the best goldfish breeding website and products in the world, you are never going to make as much money as you would if you had built a well-executed website about aquariums and fishkeeping. By choosing a larger market, you have more room to grow and a potentially higher ceiling on the maximum size of your business.

I know a number of people who make six figures and seven figures in their internet businesses. These people aren't necessarily any smarter than anyone else, but they do attack bigger markets. They use many of the same marketing and growth strategies that others do in their businesses, but get better results because there are many more potential customers in their market. If you find a marketing strategy that works well, you'll make a lot more money applying that strategy to a market of 20 million people than you will to a market of 2 million people.

I chose "stock research" as my niche in part because of the size of the market. Around 55 percent of Americans have some money invested in the stock market (http://www.gallup.com/poll/182816/little-change-percentage-americans-invested-market.aspx) and 7 percent of Americans report that they "trade stocks or other funds pretty regularly" (http://www.pewresearch.org/2007/11/19/tracking-the-traders). Assuming that my market consists only of active traders, I have around 20 million potential customers in the United States alone. While MarketBeat has grown to nearly 500,000 subscribers, I've still only scratched the surface of the market and have plenty of room for growth.

You shouldn't try to build a business that's for everyone, because you will end up with a business that doesn't really help anyone.

However, you shouldn't limit yourself to a very small section of a market either. Instead, you should choose a relatively broad category that has significant room for growth.

For example, "sports" might be too broad of a niche and "Green Bay Packers Cheerleaders" is probably too narrow of a niche. A happy medium might be writing about the NFC North division of the NFL, which consists of the Chicago Bears, Detroit Lions, Green Bay Packers, and Minnesota Vikings. That niche is narrow enough that you can cover it well, but not so narrow that you are dramatically limiting the size of your market.

Competition is a Good Thing

As you begin to evaluate different niches, you will immediately notice that there are already people creating content and selling products and services in just about every market you can think of.

If you thought you would be the first person to build a business about raising goats, gold panning equipment, weight loss through hypnosis, curing smelly feet, ninja training, pie of the month clubs, or Wizard of Oz collectibles, then you're too late. There are already competitors who are creating content and selling products in all these niches. In fact, you will likely find that there's already competition in just about every niche you're considering—and that's a good thing!

When there are already established players in a market, that only means that there are other companies making money in that market. It doesn't mean that you missed the boat and that it's too late to compete. It simply means that the commercial viability of your niche has already been proven. If people in your niche are already buying products and services from someone else, they would likely buy products and services from you, if you were to come up with something better than what exists.

Before SpaceX came onto the scene in in the mid 2000's, a joint venture between Boeing and Lockheed Martin, known as the United Launch Alliance (ULA), had a near monopoly on launching satellites into space in the United States. Elon Musk and the team at SpaceX didn't look at the commercial space launch market and give up because there was already a dominant competitor. Instead, they evaluated the space launch market, and discovered that they could significantly lower launch costs through vertical integration and by creating reusable rockets. They have gone on to win lucrative commercial cargo contracts with NASA, have more than 30 launches planned in the next four years, and are on track to start shuttling astronauts to and from the International Space Station in the years to come (http://qz.com/281619/what-it-took-for-elon-musks-spacex-to-disrupt-boeing-leapfrog-nasa-and-become-a-serious-space-company).

SpaceX did not cower and move on to a different industry that was less competitive. Instead, they embraced the competitive nature of their industry, studied the competition, outmaneuvered them, and now regularly beat ULA for space launch contracts.

When you are entering an industry that has existing players, your goal should be to learn from them and improve on their efforts, not avoid them at all costs.

MarketBeat was definitely not the first stock research website on the internet, but we were able to match our competitors' efforts and outflank them by offering the most comprehensive coverage of equities research on the web. Then, we took it a step further and created our email newsletter, which was customized to each individual subscriber's stock portfolio.

Never let competition stop you from entering a niche. You only need to develop a few small advantages over the existing competition, and a portion of the market will flock to your business.

Don't Be a "Me Too" Competitor

When you're first getting started, you probably won't know what you need to do to be successful. When you're not sure what to do, it can be very tempting to look at an existing competitor in your niche and try to replicate their success by doing what they did or copying their business outright. This almost never works.

You might not actually know *why* your competitors are successful. They could be successful because of an outside marketing strategy or internal operational effort that you are completely unaware of (and therefore unable to copy). Most people that try to copy a competitor will copy the superficial aspects of the business, such as their website, but typically aren't able to copy what actually makes them truly successful.

Avoid Dated Strategies.

You also can't go back in time and start your business when your competitors started their businesses. The strategies that worked to launch an online business in 2010 are not the same strategies that will work to launch an online business today.

Frankly, I would not be able to start MarketBeat over today using the same marketing and growth strategies. While things like podcasting and Kindle publishing worked great as marketing channels five years ago, they are now saturated and are increasingly ineffective. You simply can't copy the marketing strategies that a competitor used five to ten years ago. You need to build your own unique business using the growth strategies that are working today.

Be Yourself.

If you are trying to copy a business that revolves around an individual and their personality, you will almost certainly fail, because you can't copy someone else's personality, their work ethic, or their celebrity. Your strengths, skills, and personality are likely different than those of the person whose business model you're trying to emulate.

For example, John Lee Dumas of Entrepreneur on Fire (www.eofire.com) made a name for himself by launching the first daily podcast for entrepreneurs. He's had a ton of success and is making hundreds of thousands of dollars each month from his business. As you might expect, dozens of other people have tried to copy him by creating daily podcasts and entrepreneurial interview shows. No one has been able to replicate his success, because no one else is John Lee Dumas.

Copycat entrepreneurs can often make a reasonable facsimile of another business, but they never do it nearly as well as the business they are trying to copy—and that isn't helpful to anyone. The copycat entrepreneur misses out on the opportunity to learn and build their own real, unique business. Customers of the copycat entrepreneur are underserved because they are getting an inferior product or service. The original entrepreneur, whose business was copied, has his or her ideas ripped off and has to decide whether or not they want to take legal or other action.

Copying someone else's business doesn't do anyone any good, so just don't do it.

Find Out What You Have to Offer.

Your unique business should fit your strengths, your personality and your intellect. MarketBeat leverages my software development skills, my interest in personal finance and investing, and my ability to work with large chunks of data. It also doesn't require me to do things that I'm not particularly good at, such as person-to-person sales and public speaking. I'm also not the type of person that wants to become an internet celebrity, and the business I've chosen works well without one. The key is to build a unique business that leverages as many of your strengths and abilities as possible, and requires as few of your weaknesses.

Choose a Market with Willing Customers

Not all niches are created equal. In some niches, customers might hand over hundreds of dollars to purchase an online course without batting an eye. In others, it might be like pulling teeth to sell a $7.00 ebookebook. There are several questions that you can ask yourself to determine whether or not the customers in the niche you are considering will buy products:

- **What are the demographics of my niche?**
  Who are the people that follow your niche? How old
  are they? What kind of income do they have? Are
  they capable of spending money on my products and
  services if they want to buy them? If your potential
  audience is pre-teen girls or homeless people, you're
  going to have a tough time selling anything, because
  those demographics don't have a disposable income.
  On the other hand, if your audience consists of upper-
  middle-class individuals or lottery winners, you don't
  have to worry about whether or not they will be able to
  afford your products and services.

- **Are people in my niche already buying products
  from someone else?**
  If there are already products and services in your
  niche that people are buying regularly, then you know
  that they would probably be willing to buy products
  and services from you, especially if you come up with
  a better product or service. If no one is successfully
  selling anything in your space, take that as the major
  red flag that it is. If competitors are selling products
  and services in your space, pay special attention to the
  price points so that you know what kind of revenue
  opportunity exists in your potential niche.

- **What kind of benefits will my audience gain from
  buying my products?**
  If your audience will make money, save money, or
  save time by implementing the knowledge offered by
  your products and services, your sales pitch becomes
  much easier. Most people would happily pay $500.00
  for a course if they know that they were going to earn
  five times that much money by implementing what
  they learn over time. I once paid $2,500 for an online
  course and made more than $100,000 in the following

year from what I learned. I'd buy $2,500 courses all day long if I know they are going to yield similar results.

- **Is my audience fanatical about my niche?**
There are certain markets where participants are extremely passionate and enthusiastic. They are always encouraging others to join them and spend a lot of money on products and services. For instance, *Magic: The Gathering*, a competitive card game, is a niche with a rabid fan base that is more than willing to spend money. It can cost as much as $600.00 to put together a competitive deck that will do well at tournaments (https://www.quora.com/What-is-the-average-amount-of-money-per-month-spent-by-an-avid-Magic-The-Gathering-player). If someone is willing to spend $600.00 on what is essentially a deck of cards, you know that is going to be a profitable niche.

Your business ultimately has to make money by selling your own products to your customers, or by selling someone else's products to your audience through advertising. If the people in your audience are unwilling or highly resistant to purchasing products and services, you should probably find another niche. If people in your niche are more than willing to buy products and services that you might sell through your business, you know you're on the right track.

Choose a Market with Advertising Demand

You also need to know whether or not there are companies that are interested in advertising to audiences like yours. If there is a healthy level of demand for advertising space in your niche from advertisers, you will have a much easier time making money. When there are more advertisers competing for ad placements on your website through Google AdSense or another advertising network, the average cost per click (CPC) to the advertiser will rise.

Here are the top twenty most expensive keywords to target using Google AdWords, according to WordStream.com (http://www.wordstream.com/articles/most-expensive-keywords).

- Insurance
- Loans
- Mortgage
- Attorney
- Credit
- Lawyer
- Donate
- Degree
- Hosting
- Claim
- Conference Call
- Trading
- Software
- Recovery
- Transfer
- Gas/Electricity
- Classes
- Rehab
- Treatment
- Cord Blood

Certain niches consistently demand high CPCs because of the profitability of selling products and services in those niches. Keywords in financial, legal, medical, and business services consistently generate above-average CPCs for publishers in those niches.

For example, there are keywords associated with the form of cancer known as mesothelioma that command more than $100.00 per click (http://grepwords.com/1000000-top-high-paying-cpc-adwords-adsense-keywords-2015). While this sounds like an outrageous amount of money to pay for a single click, law firms that operate in this space can make a killing by suing companies on behalf of people that were exposed to asbestos and developed the cancer.

The average mesothelioma trial award is $2.4 million (http://www.asbestos.com/mesothelioma-lawyer/settlements.php), and the law firms representing the plaintiff keep a significant portion of that money. If you were a lawyer that represented mesothelioma patients and you knew that one out of every 250 clicks would result in a new client that had a strong likelihood of getting a seven-figure settlement, you would pay $100.00 per click all day long.

There are a number of ways that you can determine whether or not there is strong interest from advertisers in your niche. Here are the steps that you should take to gauge advertiser demand in your niche:

- **Perform Google Searches** – Make a list of keywords that people in your niche might search for on Google. If your niche is pet care, you might search for words like dog toys, dog facts, dog food, and dog breeds. Do a Google search for those keywords. If you search for your keywords and there are always three or four ads on the top and bottom of the page, there is very healthy demand among advertisers for your niche. If you don't see any ads in Google when you search for relevant keywords, consider that a possible red flag that there may not be strong advertiser interest in your niche.

- **Look For Affiliate Programs** – Look for products and services that you can promote on various affiliate networks, like CJ Affiliate (www.cj.com), LinkShare, (www.linkshare.com), ClickBank (www.clickbank.com) and ShareASale (www.shareasale.com). You can also do web searches for phrases like "dog food affiliate program" to help determine what affiliate networks have relevant offers in your niche. If there are a number of programs that target your niche, this is a good sign that there's advertiser demand. Take note of the relevant affiliate offers that you find, as you might be interested in promoting these offers to your audience later.

- **Look on Competitor Websites** – Find other websites in your niche and take a close look at what kind of advertisements they are running (if any). Make sure to visit these sites in a private or incognito browser, so that no ads are shown based on your past behavior. If they are running an ad network, like Google AdSense, and their website is displaying ads relevant to their niche, this is a good sign of healthy advertiser interest. However, if generic ads that aren't directly related to their niche are displaying, that might mean that no relevant ads are available. Again, take note of the products and services being promoted on your competitors' websites, because you may be interested in promoting those same products and services in the future.

If you want to determine what kind of advertising revenue you might be able to generate from your website, head on over to the Google Keyword Planner (https://adwords.google.com/KeywordPlanner). You will need a Google AdWords account to use this tool.

Enter keywords relevant to your niche and perform a search. Look at the suggested bid column and make a note of the cost-per-click amount for 10 to 20 relevant keywords for your niche. Then calculate the average of those amounts. This is an approximation of what advertisers will pay Google for each ad click on your future site. Since ad networks typically take a 30 to 40 percent cut of what an advertiser pays, make sure to reduce your average CPC calculation by that much. That means if advertisers pay an average CPC of $1.00, you'll earn about $0.65 for that click.

Once you approximate what you will earn for each click, you can make an estimate of what you will earn through Google AdSense for every 1,000 visitors to your website. Assuming that your website has a 2.5 percent click-through rate, you will earn about $16.25 for every 1,000 people that visit your website, using the above CPC example. Please note that your click through rate (CTR) may be as low as 1% or as high as 5%, depending on how you position your ads and where your web traffic is coming from.

These calculations provide a very rough estimate of what you might be able to make. There will likely be a significant variance in what you actually earn depending on advertiser demand, your ad placements, your traffic sources, and a variety of other factors.

Don't Get Stuck on Keyword Research

Many other resources that talk about niche selection suggest that you choose a niche based on whether or not you can rank in Google for keywords in that niche. The idea is that if you choose a niche with low competition and high-search-volume keywords, you will have an easier time ranking in Google's search results and getting traffic.

While keyword research can help determine whether or not there's advertiser demand in your niche, it should never be the basis of your decision-making process.

You simply cannot rely on receiving free organic traffic from Google as a marketing channel anymore. While it was a relatively straightforward process to create content that ranks for specific keywords ten years ago, that's no longer the case. Google has made it increasingly difficult to manipulate search results through a variety of new algorithms that have been implemented over the last five years. You may have heard of updates like Panda, Penguin, and Pigeon, which have all attempted to prevent website publishers from manipulating search results. It's not impossible to rank for competitive keywords, but most high-volume words are dominated by a handful of companies that have a substantially better understanding of search engine optimization (SEO) than either you or I.

The most important thing to understand about your relationship with Google is that their business interests aren't aligned with your business interests. Google's business interests are creating revenue for their shareholders and building sticky products and services that people use over and over again. They aren't concerned about whether or not they send traffic to any given website.

Organic search results are increasingly being pushed aside for paid ad placements. On the first page of search results for keywords like "insurance" and "mortgages," you can no longer see organic search results without having to scroll down past numerous ads, purchased through Google AdWords. Increasingly, receiving traffic from Google will become a pay-to-play activity. The days where small publishers could rely on Google traffic as their primary marketing channel is quickly coming to an end.

Getting traffic from Google and other search engines will, of course, be one of the marketing strategies, but you shouldn't rely on it as your primary customer acquisition strategy. Too many publishers have had to shut down their businesses because they were reliant on getting search traffic and lost much of their new visitors after one of Google's many algorithm updates. Jason Calacanis's Mahalo.com laid off more than 80 people after being on the losing end of the original Panda update in 2011 (https://www.seroundtable.com/jason-calacanis-revenge-google-matt-cutts-18794.html). The company had to pivot the entire business and relaunched as Inside.com a few years later.

Many other publishers weren't so lucky. My first business, AmericanConsumerNews.com, lost much of its traffic as a result of the first Panda update, which negatively affected many personal finance bloggers like myself. We eventually had to shut down that business after seeing our traffic decline by more than 60 percent overnight.

As you build your business, think of receiving traffic from Google and other search engines as gravy. It's nice to have, you might try to get some of it by doing basic SEO, and you'll certainly take it as long as they want to send traffic your way; but it should never be your primary traffic source or be the basis of your business. Instead, focus on using a combination of different marketing channels, like email, Bing, YouTube, podcasting, Pinterest, Facebook, Instagram, Amazon's Kindle Store, Twitter, and paid advertising techniques.

How to Identify Possible Niches

If you're still having trouble coming up with ideas for potential niches, there are several strategies you can use:

- **Consider Your Hobbies** – What are your hobbies? What do you do during your free time? Many people have successfully built businesses around their hobbies, so don't automatically assume that you can't monetize yours. There are people that make money by playing video games all day and streaming them for others to watch, so there's probably a way for you to make money from your hobby, too.

- **Review Your Work Experience** – What do you do for a day job? What are you particularly good at? Is there anything that you have personal work experience with that could become your niche?

- **Check Your Bookmarks** – There's a pretty good chance that the websites you visit most often are bookmarked in your web browser. If there are multiple websites that you have bookmarked that are in similar niches, that's a pretty good indication it's a niche you should consider.

- **Look at the Media You Consume** – What kind of books do you read? Do you listen to any podcasts? What television shows do you watch? Are there any common themes among the books, TV shows, and podcasts that you consume?

- **Review Example Lists** – Perform a Google Search for "niche ideas" and similar keywords. There are dozens of different lists of niches that people have published online. Scan through these lists to see if there's anything that interests you.

Examples of Niches

In order to kickstart your thought process, I've compiled a list of more than 100 niche ideas to help get your creative juices flowing. Please note that I haven't done any research as to whether or not these are good niches! They are simply included to help give you ideas for the types of businesses that you could build a niche around.

1. AC Compressors
2. Adoption

3. Air Hockey

4. Alternators

5. Ameraucana Chickens

6. Amino Acids

7. Animation

8. Antiques

9. Aquarium Supplies

10. Archery

11. Art History

12. Art Supplies

13. Artist Trading Cards

14. Astigmatism

15. Auto Tune

16. Baby Gifts

17. Baby Accessories

18. Baking Supplies

19. Balloon Animals

20. Bar Supplies

21. Baseball Jerseys

22. Basket Weaving

23. Beach Volleyball

24. Bearded Dragon

25. Best Luxury SUVs

26. Best Mascara

27. Best Mattress

28. Best Smartphone

29. Best Vacuum Cleaner

30. Blogging
31. Bocce Ball
32. Bookbinding
33. Busking
34. Calligraphy
35. Camper Vans
36. Candle Making
37. Car Auctions
38. Card Making
39. Carpentry
40. Catering Supplies
41. Cheerleading
42. Cheese Of The Month Club
43. Chicken Coop Ideas
44. Cliff Diving
45. Cricket
46. Crochet
47. Death In The Family
48. Dog Sledding
49. Earthenware
50. Email Marketing Services
51. Eye Floaters
52. Fencing
53. First Aid
54. Floral Design
55. Fly Fishing
56. Garden Tractor

57. Gun Safety
58. Hiccups
59. Home Brewing
60. Hot Sauce
61. How To Build A Computer
62. Insomnia
63. John Deere Lawn Mowers
64. Judo
65. Juggling
66. Knitting
67. Lasik Eye Surgery
68. Learn To Fly
69. Marbling
70. Mosaic Tile
71. Nail Biting
72. Neck Pain
73. Office Supplies
74. Online Learning
75. Oral Health
76. Parenting
77. Parking Tickets
78. Photography
79. Piano Lessons
80. Pool Supplies
81. Protein Bars
82. Restless Legs
83. Roller Skating

84. RV Accessories
85. School Supplies
86. Sculpture
87. Shyness
88. Skateboarding
89. Soap-Making Recipes
90. Squash
91. Stained Glass
92. Stamping
93. Stand Up Comedy
94. Tea Infuser
95. Tennis
96. Terracotta
97. Theatre
98. Tinnitus
99. Trampolining
100. Trapping
101. Tug of War
102. Unemployment
103. Violin Lessons
104. Vision Therapy
105. Water Polo
106. Wearable Technology
107. Weaving
108. Web Traffic
109. Welding Supplies
110. What Do Chickens Eat

111. Wheelchair Basketball

112. Wind

113. Yachting

114. Yam

115. Zero Turn Mowers

Avoid Analysis Paralysis

Many people get stuck at the niche selection phase when launching their business. Some are afraid that they will choose the wrong niche, so they end up making no decision at all. Their hopes and dreams are dashed before the business even exists.

The key to actually making a decision and choosing a niche is to give yourself a deadline. If you are serious about launching a business, commit to choosing your niche within the next seven days. In seven days' time, you should be able to consider several dozen different niches, narrow them down, and evaluate your top choices based on the criteria outlined in this chapter.

How to Select Your Niche in the Next Seven Days

If you are ready to take action and start your authority publishing business, begin by brainstorming as many different niche ideas as you can think of. Try to come up with at least 25 different potential niche ideas that you could pursue. Once you've made a list of ideas, narrow it down to the 10 that you are most excited about. You can use this decision matrix to determine which ideas you should pursue.

Rank each idea in the following categories from 1 to 10, using the table below:

- **Personal Passion** – How excited am I about pursuing this niche? The idea that you are most excited about should receive a 10, and the idea that you are least excited about should receive a 1.

- **Personal Experience** – What experience do I have with this niche? The idea that you have the most experience with should receive a 10, and the idea that you have the least experience with should receive a 1.

- **Current Competition** – Is this a proven market? Are there already people making money in this niche? The idea that has the most established players should receive a 10, and the idea that has the fewest competitors should receive a 1.

- **Advertiser Demand** – Is there healthy advertiser demand for this niche? What are the average CPCs for keywords in this market? The idea that has the highest average CPC should receive a 10, and the idea that has the lowest average CPC should receive a 1.

- **Revenue Potential** – How big of a market is this niche? How much money do I think I can make? The idea that you think has the most revenue potential should receive a 10, and the idea that has the least revenue potential should receive a 1.

- **Ease of Marketing** – How much work will it be to get this site off the ground? Do I have some ideas about how I could promote a brand around this niche? The idea that you think will be easiest to promote and market should receive a 10, and the idea that you think will be the hardest to promote and market should receive a 1.

	Personal Passion	Personal Experience	Advertiser Demand	Competition (More is Better)	Revenue Potential	Ease of Marketing	Total
Idea #1							
Idea #2							
Idea #3							
Idea #4							
Idea #5							
Idea #6							
Idea #7							
Idea #8							
Idea #9							
Idea #10							

Once you have ranked your 10 ideas by each of the six listed categories, total the scores. The two or three ideas that receive the highest scores are the ones you should focus on. Since some of these numbers are subjective, you shouldn't automatically choose the idea that has the highest score.

Don't Try to Pursue Two Niches at Once

If you have a hard time narrowing your choice down to a single niche, you might be tempted to try to launch in two different niches at once. But launching your own business requires a substantial amount of time, energy, and hard work. You probably won't have much success if your efforts are divided. While many successful entrepreneurs run multiple businesses, they never try to launch two different major projects at once.

Choose the single project that you are most excited about and make that your focus. You can always come back to the ideas that you passed over later.

Action Steps

- Commit to choosing your niche within the next seven days.
- Make a list of 25 different potential niches you could pursue.
- Narrow that list down to the 10 ideas that you are most excited about.
- Evaluate your 10 niche ideas, using the decision matrix in this chapter.
- Select the best one for you, and begin building your online business.

CHAPTER TWO

*Choosing A Name
for Your Business*

PICKING THE NAME FOR your business can feel like a daunting task. You want to choose the perfect name and create a great brand that your audience will love. However, a dilemma awaits. Either you will have trouble coming up with any good name ideas, or you will have far too many name ideas, and won't be able to narrow them down to one winner. It is easy to get stuck at this phase of launching a business because you can't make a decision.

Fortunately, choosing a good name doesn't have to be so hard. By learning what actually makes a good name and how to brainstorm good name ideas, you will be able to choose a name for your business in no time.

In this chapter, you will learn:

- The characteristics of a good business name.
- Different strategies you can use to come up with names for your business.
- How to find a domain name for your business that isn't already taken.
- How to check whether or not someone is using the name you have selected.
- How to narrow down your ideas to a single winning brand name.
- How to get a logo designed for your business.

Two Strategies for Naming Your Brand

There are two schools of thought for choosing a name.

Industry-centric Brand Names

First, you can choose a name that represents what your business does. Businesses like Bank of America, Ford Motor Co., Home Depot, UnitedHealth Group, and AT&T (originally American Telephone & Telegraph) use this strategy. When you hear the name of one of these businesses, you immediately recognize what industry the business is in and what the business probably does. The primary benefit of this strategy is that you don't need to teach your customers what your brand is about. For example, at USGolfTV, it's immediately clear to our viewers and our readers that we produce golf video and content in the United States. The downside is that it can be harder to build a very unique brand if your business has a generic name.

The Innovative Outsider Angle

The other strategy is to make up a new name and build a brand around it. This doesn't necessarily mean the name of your business is a word that no one has ever heard of before, but it does mean that no one else has used it in your industry. For example, the word "apple" has been around since the dawn of the English language, but it wasn't until Steve Jobs and Steve Wozniak founded Apple Inc. that the word "apple" meant anything in the computer industry. Some companies that use the new name strategy include Walmart, Exxon Mobil, Verizon, Kroger, Amazon, Boeing, Wells Fargo, and Procter & Gamble. The two main benefits of using this strategy is that you have the opportunity to define the meaning of your brand and you can be certain that no one else is using your name. The downside is that you have to start your marketing process by educating your audience on what your brand means, which can cost both time and money.

Industry-centric Equals Efficiency

While both of these naming strategies are viable for your online authority publishing business, I tend to lean toward choosing a business name that makes it immediately clear what the business does. You also don't have to spend precious ad dollars educating your audience about what your brand means and can instead direct that money toward advertising, which directly generates sales. It's also statistically unlikely that, as an online entrepreneur, your business will ever become a billion-dollar brand, so it's all right if you miss out on some of the branding opportunities that having a totally unique name affords.

What Makes a Good Name

The criteria that make for a good brand name can be somewhat difficult to define. While we can often recognize

and name when we hear it, it can be challenging to
ate why that particular brand name is effective. As
the research for this chapter, I went through and reviewed the names of hundreds of major brands and found a few
commonalities that make for a great brand name.

While these guidelines are not universal, many good brand
names meet the following criteria:

- **Short and Concise** – Good brand names tend to
  be short brand names. The names of Fortune 500
  companies tend to be between two and five syllables
  long. Try to avoid any brand name that's longer than
  five syllables, because these names tend to be harder
  to communicate to your potential customers.

- **Memorable** – The name of your business should be
  memorable to everyone. You should be able to tell
  someone the name of your business and they should
  be able to recall it 48 hours later. If you want to test
  whether or not your name idea is memorable, call five
  of your friends and mention it in passing. Two days
  later, call them back up and ask them if they remember
  what the name of your business is. If they remember
  it accurately, you know that your name passes the
  memorability test.

- **Easy to Pronounce** – Good brand names tend to
  smoothly roll off your tongue. If your name is difficult
  to pronounce, it will also be difficult to remember.
  Try to say the name of your business idea 10 times
  in rapid succession. If repeating the name of your
  business ten times fast becomes a tongue twister, you
  might want to consider a smoother-sounding name for
  your online business.

- **Defines What Your Business Does** – I truly believe
  that the best brand names inherently define what

your business does. If you can identify a concise, memorable, and easy-to-pronounce name that also defines what your business does, you know you have a winner.

How to Come up with Name Ideas

There is no step-by-step process that will guarantee that you come up with a good name idea. You might come up with a bunch of name ideas during a brainstorming session. You might get a great name idea from a friend, a coworker, or someone on Facebook. The name idea you end up using might come to you in the shower, while your subconscious is doing the thinking for you. There might even be a business in a different industry whose name you like and want to create a variation of for your own business. While there's no surefire way to find the perfect name idea, there is an exercise that you can do that will help get your mental juices flowing.

This exercise, which I like to refer to as word crunching, involves coming up with words that are used in your industry, and combining them with other words, in hopes of coming up with name ideas.

The first step is to think of all of the words that describe your niche. In the investing world, I would list words like stocks, bonds, mutual funds, investing, markets, Wall Street, and trading. Once you have run out of ideas, run each word through Thesaurus.com to get additional ideas for words that describe your niche. Ideally, you'll have as many as 20 different words that you could potentially use as part of your business name.

The next step is to look up a list of common prefixes and suffixes on the internet. Prefixes and suffixes are simply words that you attach to the beginning or the end of one of the words that are used to describe your industry. You can find a number of good lists of prefixes and suffixes by searching for "domain prefixes list" and "domain suffixes list" on Google. Lean Domain Search has made a list of the 5,000 most commonly used domain prefixes and suffixes at http://www.leandomainsearch. com/top-domain-name-prefixes-and-suffixes. Some common suffixes include words like blog, guide, advice, info, hq, report, journey, and tutorial.

After you have a list of industry words and a list of common suffixes and prefixes, start combining industry words with either a prefix or a suffix to come up with name ideas. For my investing example, you might come up with names like MarketBlog, WallStreet Guide, Trading Advice, Market Info, StocksHQ, Wall-Street Report, Investor's Journey, or Trading Tutorial. Spend 30 minutes coming up with as many combinations as you can, then choose the five to 10 names that you like the most. You might immediately find a winning name in that list. You also might have a list of decent names to choose from or you might not have any good names in the bunch at all. Again, there's no perfect process to choose a name for your business. You just have to keep mulling over ideas until the right name shows up.

How to Choose Between Multiple Name Ideas

If you are trying to decide between multiple name ideas, there are several things that you can do to narrow the list down to a single choice:

- **Check Your Ideas Against the "What Makes a Good Name" Criteria** – Earlier in the chapter, there's a list of criteria for what makes a good name. For each name idea, verify that it is short and concise, memorable, easy to pronounce, and defines what your business does.

- **Conduct a Facebook Poll** – In any Facebook group that you are a part of, you can create a poll of different name ideas. Have the other people in the group vote on your list of name ideas to get some public feedback. It often works well to poll various business groups that you might be a part of. If you're not part of a group, you can post the question on your personal Facebook profile, but you will just have to ask respondents to comment their choice since polls aren't currently available on personal Facebook profiles.

- **Create a PickFu Poll** – For a small fee, PickFu (www.pickfu.com) allows you to poll their network of respondents for feedback on your name ideas. Using their service, you can create a poll that lists all your name ideas, and they will have several dozen respondents choose which of your name ideas they like best. The respondents will also provide you feedback, including why they might like one name idea over another.

Verify No One Else Owns Your Name Idea

Once you have found a name idea that you like, you will need to make sure that it's not already taken by someone else. If the name of your business is already being used by a prominent website, blog, or company, you should move on to another idea. At the very least, using a name that's been taken by someone else will create confusion among your customers and the customers of the other business that has the same name. One of your readers might do a Google search for your website and land on your competitor's website instead!

Worst case scenario, you might find yourself on the end of a trademark infringement lawsuit for using someone else's registered trademark, which will cost you thousands of dollars in legal fees and hundreds of hours of lost time that could have gone into growing your business.

First, do a basic trademark search to make sure that no one else has registered your business name as a trademark. You can do a basic trademark search on the U.S. Patent & Trademark Office website at http://www.uspto.gov/trademarks-application-process/search-trademark-database. Search for your name idea and make sure there aren't any listings for the name you want to use. If there are listings for your name, you may still be able to use the name if the registration is dead or if the registration is in a different category than your business. However, you will want to buy an hour of a trademark lawyer's time to be sure that you won't run into trouble for using the name.

Before I went full time with my business, I worked at a website design agency that had gone under a merger with another firm. They chose a good name for the combined business, but failed to do a basic trademark search for the name they had chosen. They had developed a logo, a website, and an entirely new brand around their new name. A couple of months later, they received a cease and desist letter from the company that owned the trademark. They ended up having to change the name of the business again, and redid all the branding work for their *new* new name. Many customers were confused about the multiple name changes and it ended up being a big hassle for the business. This headache could have been avoided if they had done a basic trademark search for the name they wanted to use and had seen that it was already taken.

The second step to make sure that your name idea isn't taken is to perform a basic Google search for the name you want to use. If there's an established website, blog, or business that is already using your name idea, you should probably move on to your next name idea. When someone searches for your name in Google, the established competitor will almost certainly outrank your website. In order to avoid confusion and to establish your own unique brand, I recommend only choosing a brand name that is not currently being used by anyone else.

Don't Worry If You Can't Get the .Com

All of the good dot com domain names are already taken. Domain squatters have gone through and registered every dictionary word, almost every combination of dictionary words and almost every combination of three, four and five letters and numbers under the .com domain extension. If you want to get a dotcom domain name, you will have to either purchase a good domain name off of a marketplace like SEDO.com or be incredibly creative about the domain name you choose. I don't recommend doing either, because domains that sell on the secondary market tend to be expensive, and any open domain name that you are able to find will probably include creative spellings, hyphens, numbers, or other elements that will be hard for your customers to remember.

Instead of futilely searching for a .com domain name that probably doesn't exist, I suggest building a brand using a domain that's listed under one of the hundreds of new top level domains (TLDs). There are now more than 1,300 .com alternatives that you can use for your domain name. Individuals have been able to register domains under alternative TLDs like .net, .org, .us, .info, .biz and .co for quite a while. Now, there are a whole host of new extensions to choose from. While there are far too many to list here, some of the popular new extensions include .xyz, .top, .win, .club, .site, .bid, .link, .red, .online, .vip, .loan, .science, .party, .click, .website, .space, .tech, .lol, .review, .work, .trade and .news. For a complete list of available TLDs, visit www.namestat.org.

The .com domain extension still tends to be the standard extension that most businesses use, but many new companies are using .co, .io and other TLDs, such as CodePen.io, Gleam. IO and Angular.io.

Over time, it will be increasingly common for blogs and websites to use any number of different TLDs. There are already

ıan 6 million .xyz domains available, and that number is
ıg by thousands of new domains every day.

Focus on some of the new extensions that are gaining popularity, such as .co, .io, .xyz, .top, .win, .club and .site. You can always go back and pay five figures for the .com domain name you actually want down the line as your business becomes successful, but paying a lot of money for a domain name typically isn't a good investment early on in your business.

Should Your Name Be Your Brand?

Some online entrepreneurs actively work to build a brand around their name. They portray themselves as subject matter experts and teach their readers about relevant topics through blog posts, podcasts, books and public speaking. Their personal brand and their business brand become inexorably linked and they become internet celebrities of sorts. These internet celebrities are able to leverage the name that they build for themselves to land bigger speaking gigs at conferences and huge book deals. They also create products to sell to their audiences, and make money by recommending other people's products that pay affiliate commissions.

A quintessential example of this branding strategy in the internet business space is Pat Flynn (www.smartpassiveincome.com). He has established himself as an authority and an expert in online business through his blog, his podcasts, his public speaking, and his book.

He started his blog in 2008 after being laid off as an architect and gained notoriety after he started creating a monthly report of the income he was making from his online businesses. Every month, Flynn makes more than $100,000 in affiliate commissions by endorsing other people's products and services. He has also effectively leveraged his personal brand to land speaking gigs at conferences and other events.

While I have a ton of respect for people like Pat Flynn, who have built audiences around a compelling personal brand, their branding strategy is not what I personally want to create. I have built an audience of nearly 500,000 email subscribers, but you won't see my face or my name prominently featured on any of the businesses that I run. I could sell any of my companies tomorrow and very few of my customers would even notice. I'm not trying to be totally anonymous in any of my businesses, but there are some very good reasons to separate your personal brand from your business brand.

Here are a few reasons why your personal brand should never become your business:

- **You get stuck on a hamster wheel of content creation.** When you build an internet business based around your personal brand, your ability to generate income is tied directly to you producing content on an ongoing basis. If you stop creating new content (blogs, podcasts, etc.), people will stop coming. Your audience will expect you to continue to produce content at the same rate you have been, and likely won't accept content from a writer that you hire, because they want to learn from you and not one of your employees. If you don't meet their expectations, they will go somewhere else. That means you need to continue to produce content regardless of whether you're motivated to do so, and whether or not you actually have something new or interesting to say.

- **You can never sell your business.** Whenever a radio host stops personally doing their show, the show is almost always scrapped entirely and replaced with a different program. Without the host, there is no show. The same is true for your personality-driven business. The value of your business is the goodwill that you've built up with your audience throughout the years. If you're not there, that goodwill disappears. When your personal brand is the core of your business, it can't be transferred to anyone else without losing a significant share of the audience. This makes it almost impossible to sell your business in the event that you want to move onto another project.

- **It's very difficult to start doing something different.** You and the personal brand that you create are inexorably linked. If you become known as the girl or guy who is the expert on earning airline miles and you make a great income doing that, you'll have a hard time transitioning if you ever want to do something else. You might decide that you're sick of writing about airline loyalty programs every day, but your audience's attention is tied to you writing about miles and points. If you want to make something else your primary focus, you'll essentially have to start over with a new audience on a different topic.

- **You can't systematize or delegate your business.** In normal businesses, you can always bring on new team members or systems to improve how work gets done. When your personal brand and your business's brand are closely linked, people will expect to be reading and listening to content directly produced by you. Your audience will want to read emails, articles and tweets written by you, not your virtual assistant or one of your employees. You can certainly bring on team members to help, but you will never be able to build a team that fully takes over the day-to-day operations of your business.

Focus on Your Audience

Instead of making your personal brand the focus of your business, try to make your readers the focus. Your writing style should focus on how your products, services and content impacts and benefits your readers. Instead of telling your readers, "Come, learn from me. I'm an expert," the message should be "Here's an incredibly helpful service or piece of content for you."

By separating your personal brand and your business, you have the freedom to be able to sell if you choose. You are not tied to personally creating content on a weekly basis over the long term because you can always hire someone else to create content. Finally, you can delegate, automate, and outsource tasks that you don't want to do, because your readers won't be expecting your personal touch on everything your business does.

How to Recover from a Bad Name Choice

When I first launched MarketBeat in 2011, the business was called Analyst Ratings Network. I chose that name because I wanted to highlight the fact that we offered the most comprehensive coverage of analysts' recommendations on the web. I never thought it was a perfect name, but it kind of made sense given the kind of information that we offered at the time and the domain name that was available (analystratings.net). I thought Analyst Ratings Network was the best name we could get, given how many other financial publications and trademarks in the financial space already exist. Surprisingly, the name www.analystratings.net wasn't taken, so we snatched it up and used it as our primary domain.

Over time, we expanded the service to offer much more financial information besides equities research, and the name made less sense as it no longer adequately communicated what we did. It wasn't until I attended an entrepreneurship conference in April 2015 that I knew the name needed to be changed. A number of people asked about my business and whenever anyone tried to repeat the name back to me, it almost always came back as "Analyst Network" or something else that was totally inaccurate. Good brand names must be memorable and describe what your business actually does. Analyst Ratings Network failed on both of those qualifications. I decided it was time for a rebrand.

At first, I thought it would be incredibly difficult to pull off a rebrand. We have several hundred thousand people that read our content, numerous advertisers, and business partners that would all have to know about the change. We also had the basic challenge of coming up with a whole new name.

We ended up finding the name MarketBeat for sale on SEDO for $10,000. I figured that name would have been trademarked, but the only trademarks were long expired. We ended up buying MarketBeat.com, MarketBeat.Net, and MarketBeat.org for around $12,000 in total. We also got a go-ahead from our lawyer telling us it was safe to use the name, so we were free to move forward.

We had a new logo designed by a local infographic design agency called Lemonly (www.lemonly.com). Once we had the logo and branding material in hand, we set a switch-over date of June 1st, 2015. We immediately informed everyone we did business with of the name change via email, including advertisers, business partners, friendly competitors, contractors, and anyone else that had helped grow the business in any way. We also sent a series of emails to our entire mailing list prior to the switch-over. We put notices in our daily newsletter and on the homepage of our website. The goal was to make sure that the name change was impossible for our readers to miss. We spent the entire month of May making sure everyone knew that we were about to change.

When the big launch day arrived, the name change was a total non-event. There wasn't widespread confusion about what happened to Analyst Ratings Network. Because we over-communicated the change, the immediate transition was almost entirely painless. For the following six months after launch, we included both the old name and the new name in our emails so that anyone that missed our onslaught of communication pieces would understand what had happened. We also left the notification on our website for several months after the change. We kept using the old business name on our existing customers' credit card statements so that they didn't accidentally think that someone had stolen their credit card number. We also did a 301 redirect so that our old website URL automatically redirected users to our new website.

Initially, I thought it would be almost impossible for an established brand like Analyst Ratings Network to switch names. It turns out that changing the name of your business isn't that big of a deal, as long as you communicate it to your readers well. If you find yourself with a business name that doesn't make sense anymore, don't believe that you are stuck with the name you have. It is possible to transition to an entirely new brand without losing customers, losing advertisers, or having any significant adverse effect on your business.

How to Get Your Business Logo Designed

Before you launch your business, you will probably want to have a logo made for your brand. You should have some kind of logo on your website, but don't focus too heavily on it early on. People aren't going to read your content, subscribe to your email list, and continue to follow your brand because they like your logo. They are going to stick around because they love your content and what you have to say. Your content and the value you provide should always take precedence over secondary issues, like your logo and the design of your website.

There are several different ways that you can have a logo designed for your business. Unless you are a graphic designer, you should probably not try to create a logo yourself.

so recommend against having a friend or an acquain-
create a logo for you. If they end up creating something
that you hate, you'll have to use the logo anyway to avoid hurting
their feelings, or you'll have to tell them that the logo they made
isn't very good.

Here are some different ways that you can get a logo made
at different price points:

- **Fiverr.com** – The cheapest way to have a logo made is
  using Fiverr.com. There are a number of freelancers
  that have created listings on Fiverr, known as gigs,
  where they will create a logo for you for as little as
  $5.00. While the base price of every gig is $5.00, you
  will probably have to pay between $25.00 and $50.00
  to get a high-resolution version of your logo, along with
  all of the source files. Make sure to read the reviews
  of any gig you purchase, because the quality will vary
  dramatically from gig to gig. At this price point, you
  also need to watch out for sellers who send plagiarized
  logos, which could leave you on the hook for copyright
  infringement.

- **Create a Logo Contest** – You can use either
  DesignContest.com or 99Designs.com to create a logo
  design contest where freelancer designers will develop
  logo concepts for you on spec. For around $300 you
  can create a request on Design Contest or 99Designs,
  and receive between 25 or 50 different submissions
  to choose from. This can be a slightly-more-expensive,
  but still cost-effective option for many entrepreneurs,
  because you only pay for the logo that you choose.
  The only downside is that you often can't go through
  multiple revisions of the logo with your designer
  to create the perfect one. You can usually provide
  feedback about designs during the contest which may
  spur additional entries, but don't expect a back-and-

forth conversation with the designers competing in your contest.

- **Hire a Local Graphic Designer** – If you live in a community of 50,000 people or more, there are almost certainly freelance graphic designers that you can hire to create a logo for you. You can often find them at local meetup groups and events, or through their personal websites. For between $500 and $1,000, you can typically hire a local designer to create five to 10 logo concepts for you. You can choose the one that you like the most and work with the designer to tweak it until you like it. This can be a great option if you find a designer whose portfolio you like and your budget allows for. Your designer may also be able to help you design and customize your website for an additional fee.

- **Use a Freelance Job Posting Site** – If you can't find a good designer locally and don't want to use Fiverr or a logo design contest, you can use services like Upwork. com or Freelancer.com to find someone to create the logo and branding for your business. While you will find many good designers that will create a logo for you for an hourly rate, be mindful of the fees that these services tack on to the freelancer's hourly rate.

Regardless of how you have your logo built, there are several things you need to ensure your designer provides along with your logo:

- **Color Scheme** – Make sure to get a list of colors used in the logo in hexadecimal format (often referred to as hex colors). You will need these for the design of your website. If your logo designer doesn't provide these, you can extract them using PhotoShop or Paint Shop Pro later, and try to make a color scheme based off that information. The better way to go is to just ask your logo designer for a color scheme that you can use for your website from the start.

- **Source/Vector File** – This is a version of your logo that contains all of the source elements that were used to create your file, such as design elements, fonts, and text. If you ever want to make changes to your logo in the future, having the source file available will make editing your logo file much easier. Source files are often provided in Adobe Illustrator (.ai) or Adobe PhotoShop (.psd) formats.

- **High Resolution File** – A high resolution of your logo is necessary so that you can use your logo in a variety of contexts. While smaller images are more than sufficient for web use, you will want a high resolution version of your logo (at least 2,000 pixels by 2,000 pixels) in the event that you ever want to use your logo in print. Otherwise, the image may get blurry or distorted when it is stretched. If you have a source or a vector file, you may not need your designer to provide a high-resolution version of your image because a high-resolution logo can be created from the source files.

- **Ownership Rights** – Be clear with the designer you are working with that you are paying them on a "work for hire" basis, and that you will maintain all ownership rights to the logo that they are creating for you when the work is done.

Action Steps

- Choose what name you want to use for your brand.
- Verify that no one else is using the name you have selected.

- Verify that your brand name has not been registered as a trademark by anyone else.

- Register a domain name for the brand that you want to use.

- Have a logo created for your brand.

CHAPTER THREE

Launching Your Website

THIS IS WHERE THE rubber meets the road. You have chosen your target market, developed a name, and created a visual brand for your business. Now, you are ready to begin building your website, which will serve as the hub for everything that your business does online.

Your website will be home for the content that you produce, will act as the sales platform for the products and services that you sell, and will allow you to collect email addresses to build your mailing list. You will be active on a variety of social networks like Facebook, Twitter, Instagram, and Snapchat, but the goal should always be to drive people back to your website so that they can engage with your content, sign up for your email list, click on ads on your website, and buy your products.

In this chapter, you will learn:

- How to select a high-quality web hosting company.
- Why WordPress is the only software you should use to build your website.
- How to choose a theme for your website.
- What plugins every website owner should set up on their WordPress website.
- How to get technical help with your website.
- How to plan for the launch of your website.

If you already know how to build a website or have other technical skills, much of this chapter might seem rather basic to you. If this is the case, feel free to scan through or skip the parts you already know.

If you haven't built a website before, the content in this chapter may seem difficult to grasp initially. If that's the case, lean on the resources mentioned along the way, and don't be afraid to get help from someone that already knows how to build a WordPress website. Your website is one of the most important pieces of your online business, and you don't want to mess around with it too much if you don't know what you are doing.

How to Choose a Web Hosting Company

In order to launch your website, you will need a basic web hosting account to provide the technology and infrastructure. Your web host may also register your domain name for you, provide a customized email account that matches your domain, and offer other services.

You may already be aware of some well-known web hosting companies, like DreamHost, HostGator, GoDaddy and BlueHost. There are also hundreds of other smaller companies that offer website hosting that you have never heard of. Almost every web hosting company will offer a basic WordPress hosting package for between $5.00 and $20.00 per month, but the quality of service that you'll receive can vary widely from provider to provider.

When shopping for something online, your first inclination is probably to read reviews and compare prices. This is a challenging proposition for web hosting companies because the prices are extremely similar from host to host. It also doesn't help that every web hosting company in the world has a mix of both very positive and extremely negative reviews.

Some customers will never have a problem with their web host and will be more than happy with the service they receive. Other customers of the same web host might have a bunch of problems with their website and be extremely frustrated. Many review sites also receive affiliate commissions from the hosting companies they write about, so you don't know whether or not they are actually providing you their objective opinion. Review sites tend to not be very helpful in selecting a web host, and I suggest you don't try to include them as part of your decision-making progress.

In my personal experience, many of the big-name web hosting companies offer a very similar level of service at nearly identical prices. Whether you choose DreamHost, HostGator, GoDaddy, 1&1, BlueHost, Liquid Web, Media Temple or Site Ground, you'll be able to get a basic WordPress hosting account for between $5.00 and $10.00 per month. Starter hosting packages from any of these companies will be more than sufficient to get your site going.

At sub $10.00 per month prices, you probably shouldn't expect to get much in terms of technical support. Web hosting companies cannot profitably afford to provide great customer service for cheap shared hosting plans. If you are willing to pay a bit more and want better customer support, you might choose a premium WordPress hosting service like WPEngine (www.wpengine.com), which starts at $29.00 per month. Services like WPEngine tend to offer faster and more reliable hosting, as well as better customer service.

When I was first getting started, I used a basic web hosting account from DreamHost (www.dreamhost.com) which cost $8.00 per month. The best thing about their service is that they will install WordPress on your web hosting account with a single click, which can prevent some potential technical headaches. I have since had to lease a series of dedicated servers because of the large amount of traffic our websites receive, but DreamHost served my business reasonably well for the first several years of operations. I currently lease dedicated servers from Web Hosting Buzz (www.webhostingbuzz.com).

WordPress: Your Website Management Software

When I was first building websites in the mid-1990's, every line of code that made up the structure and design of your website had to be written by hand. This made building websites inaccessible to anyone without significant technical abilities. Thankfully, this is no longer the case. Through a series of initiatives, there are now software tools that allow anyone to put together a website without having to know a single line of code. This type of software—known as a content management system—runs on your web hosting account and allows you to easily manage your website and post content to it, without any coding experience.

WordPress (www.wordpress.org) is the single most popular content management system and it powers 26 percent of all websites on the internet as of May 2016 (http://expandedramblings.com/index.php/wordpress-statistics). More than 76.5 million blogs run on WordPress, and 50,000 new websites are launched every day. While there are a variety of other content management systems available, you should almost certainly default to WordPress because of the wide array of themes and plugins available for the platform. WordPress is also very well-suited to the type of website that you will be creating because it's relatively straightforward to set up things like ecommerce stores, landing pages, and membership sites. If you run into trouble with WordPress, it's very easy to get technical help. WordPress also happens to be free and open-source software.

The only other option that you might consider to start out with is SquareSpace (www.squarespace.com). SquareSpace's unique service combines web hosting services along with an easy-to-use content management system. SquareSpace includes a variety of themes and add-ons, but the library of available tools isn't nearly as extensive as what's available in Word-Press. SquareSpace also tends to be a bit more expensive than running a standard hosting account with a WordPress website as well. You might choose SquareSpace if you don't have much in the way of technical skills and plan on doing all of the work yourself, but your default choice should be WordPress, unless you have a compelling reason to choose SquareSpace.

Installing WordPress on Your Web Hosting Account

After you get your web hosting account set up, the first order of business is to install WordPress into your hosting account. Almost every major web hosting service will allow you to do this with a single click inside your hosting account's control panel. The easiest way to figure out how to install WordPress on your particular web host is to do a Google search for the name of your web host and the words "install WordPress." If you are unable to figure out how to install WordPress on your hosting account, email your web hosting provider's support email address, and they will often do it for you, or point you in the right direction so that you can do it yourself.

Choosing a Theme for Your Website

Once you get WordPress installed, the next step is to choose a theme for your website. Your website's theme will provide all of the visual and design elements for your website, so make sure you choose a theme you like. WordPress does include a standard default theme, but you should take the time to install a custom theme that better matches the brand you are creating. There are a number of websites which offer a directory of WordPress themes that you can use on your website. Some WordPress themes are available for free, but higher-quality and more customizable themes usually cost between $20.00 and $50.00 to use on your website.

Here is a list of theme directories you can browse:

- Creative Market – https://creativemarket.com/themes
- Color Lib – https://colorlib.com/wp/free-wordpress-themes (includes free themes)
- Elegant Themes – http://www.elegantthemes.com
- Simple Themes – https://www.simplethemes.com
- Theme Circle – http://www.themecircle.net
- Theme Forest – http://themeforest.net/category/wordpress
- WordPress.org Theme Directory – https://wordpress.org/themes (includes free themes)

When you purchase a theme or download a free theme, you will be given a .zip file that contains all the necessary elements. In order to upload and install that theme, log in to WordPress on your website.

Click on "Appearance" in the left navigation menu, then click the "Add new" button at the top of the sub-menu that pops out. On the page, in the right frame, you will see a button that says

"Upload theme". Click on that. Then, select the theme's .zip file from your computer and click the "Install now" button. After your theme has been uploaded, activate it, and your entire website will adopt your theme's look and feel.

You may want to further customize your website after installing your theme. For example, you might want to add in your own logo, change the colors, or move elements around. Most paid WordPress themes come with their own control panel that allows you to customize most elements of your theme. Look for the "Customize" or "Theme options" menu item under WordPress's appearance tab. Some themes also create their own top-level menu items in WordPress's navigation. If you want to customize something that your theme doesn't allow you to change inside of its provided control panel, you may need the help of a freelance web designer to make the changes.

Must-Have Plugins for Every WordPress Website

The features and functionality of WordPress can be expanded through the use of add-on software, known as plugins. There are plugins available that add forms to your website, prevent spammers from posting comments, add an ecommerce store, place landing pages, improve your website's search rankings, track how many people visit your website, and perform many other useful tasks.

Here are some of the plugins that I add to every WordPress website that I use:

- **Super Cache** – Super Cache will create a static copy of the pages on your website to improve performance and reduce your website's load time. Using a caching plugin like Super Cache will also allow your server to have more people on your website at the same time without slowing to a crawl.

- **Anti-Spam Bee** – WordPress includes an anti-spam plugin called Akismet by default, but I prefer Anti-Spam Bee because many spammers actively work to get around Akismet's filters. Anti-Spam Bee also has a smaller impact on page load times because it doesn't load any third-party JavaScript libraries like jQuery.

- **Clean Contact** – Clean Contact will put a basic contact form on the contact page of your website. It's lightweight and works well. If you want to include more complicated forms on your website, consider using Contact Form 7 (www.contactform7.com).

- **Google XML Sitemaps** – This plugin will create an XML sitemap that Google, Bing, and other search engines can use to make sure that they have properly indexed all of the pages on your website. After installing this plugin, make sure to submit your sitemap to Google with the Google Search Console (www.google.com/webmasters/tools) and to Bing with Bing Webmaster Tools (www.bing.com/webmaster).

- **Yoast SEO** – This plugin will take care of all of the technical optimizations you need to have your website rank well in search engines. Yoast SEO also encourages you to choose a keyword to focus on in your articles, and then makes sure that you use that keyword appropriately so that you have a better chance of ranking for it in Google and Bing.

- **Google Analytics** – Google Analytics is a free visitor tracking service from Google. By placing a snippet of code on your website, or using a Google Analytics plugin, Google will track each of your visitors, how they got to your website and what pages they viewed. Everyone hoping to sell something through their website should have Google Analytics installed, because it shows how many people are on your website and what they do when they're there.

- **Social Sharing Plugins** – There are a variety of plugins that will add social media sharing buttons to your site, which will allow readers to easily share your content on Facebook, Twitter, and other social media platforms. I have personally used the plugin Social Media Feather to add social sharing functionality to my sites, but there are many other equally good social sharing plugins available for WordPress.

- **A Backup Plugin** – Given the amount of work you're doing to build your website and fill it with valuable content, you're going to want a backup plan in case something goes wrong and your files somehow get deleted. There are many plugins that make it easy to regularly back up your files and your database of posts automatically, such as WPBackItUp. Install a backup plugin right away, even though you hope to never need to use its restore function.

These are just a few examples of the thousands of plugins that are available for WordPress. You can view a list of the most popular WordPress plugins at https://wordpress.org/plugins/browse/popular. To install one of these plugins, click the "Plugins" menu item on the left of your WordPress installation. Then, click the "Add New" button at the top and search for the name of the plugin you want to install. Click the "Install Now" button next to the plugin you want to install, then click the "Activate Plugin" link after the plugin has been installed to enable it.

Try to limit the number of plugins you install to the essentials. Installing too many plugins will slow down your website. Since 40 percent of web users will abandon a website that doesn't load in three seconds or less, it's important to make sure that your website is quick and snappy (https://blog.kissmetrics. com/loading-time). You should also delete any plugins that you aren't actively using, for both security and performance reasons. You can always go back and reinstall a plugin that you deleted if you decide that you want to use it again.

Additional Tasks to Complete Prior to Launch

At this point, all of the technical infrastructure you need for your website is in place. You have set up a copy of WordPress on your web hosting account. You have chosen a theme for your website and have installed some basic plugins to extend the functionality of your website. You have submitted your website to Google and Bing and have set up Google Analytics to track how many people visit your website.

It's now time to start filling out some of the base content for your site and complete a few other remaining tasks before launch:

- **Set Up Email Opt-In Forms** – You should start collecting email addresses on your website from day one. Set up an account with an email service provider like Drip (www.getdrip.com), MailChimp (www.mailchimp.com) or Aweber (www.aweber.com) prior to your launch, and use a plugin or service like OptinMonster (www.optinmonster.com) or SumoMe (www.sumome.com) to collect your initial opt-ins. Setting up your email service provider and creating effective opt-ins is something I cover in detail in my other book, *Email Marketing Demystified*, which is available at www.myemailmarketingbook.com.

- **Create Your Navigation Menu** – Your navigation menu is a hierarchical directory of the types of content that are available on your website. Your navigation menu should link to the important pages on your website, such as your about page, contact page, and the top-level categories that you create in WordPress. You should create a category for each subject you plan on writing about, then assign each post that you write to the appropriate category so readers can easily find the content they are most interested in.

- **Write Your About Page** – Your about page should contain the mission statement for your business, some personal information about you and your brand, and highlight some of the best content on your website. Include a picture of yourself so that readers can have a personal connection with you. This isn't the same as creating a personal brand, it is giving your random new business a face. HubSpot has put together a list of well-written about pages that are worth checking out at http://blog.hubspot.com/marketing/remarkable-about-us-page-examples.

- **Write Your Contact Page** – Your contact page contains information for people that want to get ahold of you. Include your email address, links to your social media profiles and a contact form (such as the one offered by Clean Contact). I recommend that you avoid putting your phone number and mailing address on your contact page, because there are crazy people on the internet, and you don't want to make it too easy for them to find you.

- **Write Your First Five Blog Posts** – You need to have something available for people to read when you launch your website. You can't simply publish one article and tell people to come back next week to read your next post. Put several articles on your website prior to launch, so that readers can spend some time and become further engaged with the content that you create.

- **Fill Out Your Sidebar** – Almost every WordPress theme comes with a sidebar, which is a relatively narrow column of content that sits next to the main body of each article. In your sidebar, you should place a brief bio about yourself, links to your most recent articles, any ad placements you want to include, and an email opt-in form. You can set up various sidebar elements using the built-in widget functionality that is included with WordPress. You can view how I have put the sidebar together on my personal website at www.mattpaulson.com.

- **Set Up Your Ad Placements (Optional)** – Create an account with an ad network like Google AdSense and place ad units on your website so that you can begin to generate revenue. This is not critically important to do before launching your website, but you should put up your ad units early on in the life of your website. Working with ad networks and placing ad units will be covered in detail in chapter six.

How to Get Help With WordPress

By now, you're either saying "I already know all of this stuff, let's get on to the good part!" or "This is overwhelming. I have no idea how to do any of this stuff!" If you are having trouble grasping some of the technical aspects of putting a website together, fear not. Because WordPress is the most widely used content management system on the planet, there are a ton of available resources which you can lean on to get help with WordPress.

Here are some different ways that you can get technical help with WordPress:

- **Use WordPress Tutorial Websites** –WPBeginner.com and WP101.com both offer excellent video tutorials that teach you how to do anything you would ever want to with WordPress. The official WordPress website also has an extensive lessons guide that covers the basics of how to use WordPress, available at https://codex.wordpress.org/WordPress_Lessons. There's a lot of WordPress training content available, but don't try to watch every video in a course before building your website. Practice just-in-time learning, and only watch the videos or read the lessons that are directly relevant to what you're working on right now.

- **Find a Local Meetup Group** – Many cities have local meetup groups for WordPress, website development, and general programming. You can often learn a lot about building websites by attending local meetups, listening to the presenters, and talking to other attendees. You can check to see if there is a relevant local meetup group by visiting www.meetup.com. A list of WordPress-specific meetup groups can be found at http://www.meetup.com/topics/wordpress.

- **Community Education Classes** – Many communities offer community education classes, which allow you to take classes from experts for a minimal fee (often around $25.00). Check and see if your community offers any relevant community education classes. If there is a WordPress class or a website development class, consider taking it. You'll be able to learn how to build a website in a structured environment and will have the opportunity to get personal help from somebody that knows what they're doing.

- **Find a Freelancer to Help You** – If you need someone to walk you through the basics of running a WordPress website and have them help with some parts of building it, don't be ashamed to get help from a local freelancer. You shouldn't hire a freelancer to build your entire website for you, but you can hire a freelancer to teach you how to use WordPress and rely on their expertise when you get stuck. You can find freelancers at local meetup groups, by searching for freelancers in your area on Google, or by posting an ad on Craigslist. If there is a code bootcamp in your area, reach out to the organizer and see if he or she has any students that might be able to help you out. If you can't find a local freelancer, you can find one online by using a service like Upwork.com or Freelancer.com.

- **Sign-Up for WP Curve** – WPCurve (www.wpcurve.com) is a subscription-based WordPress support service. For $79 per month, WPCurve will make their team of WordPress experts available to fix any issues that crop up on your website. They won't build you a new website from scratch, but they will do things like help you boost conversion rates, reduce your website's load times, recover from getting hacked, improve your search rankings, and help you configure plugins. You may not need this service on an ongoing basis, but it might be very helpful to have for a few months while you are getting your site off the ground.

- **Don't Hire a Marketing Agency** – It might be tempting to call in a local marketing agency and have them build your website for you, but this isn't a good plan in the beginning. While a marketing agency may build you a nice-looking website, they will never take responsibility for your website's success or lack thereof. It's important for you to learn the basics of using WordPress and operating a website. When you pay an agency, or even a freelancer, to do everything for you, you miss out on learning a critical competency that you'll need to run your online business.

Launching Your Website

After you've set up a hosting account, installed WordPress, picked out a theme, installed basic plugins, and rounded out your website with some basic content (including your first few articles), you are ready to plan your website launch.

Set a date and promote your website on all of your social media platforms on launch day. You should also make an email list of friends, family, and well-wishers. Send them an email letting them know about your new project and inviting them to join your website's mailing list. Try to have at least five articles published on your website at launch and have five more articles written, ready to publish after launch day. After your website launches, you will need to develop an ongoing content strategy (Chapter 4), a marketing plan to spread your website beyond your friends and family (Chapter 5), and a monetization plan to generate revenue (Chapters 6 and 7).

Launching your website is only the first 5 percent of your journey. Don't expect to get massive results right away—nobody is going to care about you or your website. Don't be surprised if the only people that are reading your blog when you first get started are your spouse and your parents.

Plan to write to a very small audience for at least six months before you begin to get any traction. It takes time to produce compelling content, build out a brand, and attract an audience that wants to hear what you have to say. Remember that you are playing a long-term game and building a business that will provide income for your family for the next five to ten years. While the first several months will be very slow, your business will steadily grow and pick up steam over time.

Action Steps

- Sign up for a web hosting service and install WordPress on your web hosting account.

- Choose a theme for your website and upload it to your WordPress dashboard.

- Install my list of must-have plugins.

- Complete the list of additional tasks prior to your launch.

- Launch your website.

CHAPTER FOUR

Content Strategy and Content Marketing

LET'S IMAGINE YOU'RE TAKING a trip to New York City and hope to attend a Yankees game while you're there. You thought they were playing a home game today, so you decided to head over to Yankee Stadium to grab a ticket and see the game. Instead of seeing field full of players and a large audience in the stand, there's nobody there. The place is a ghost town. It turns out they are playing an away game that day. Do you stick around and watch clips from old games on YouTube, because you wanted to see a baseball game? Of course not. You leave and find something else to do.

Your readers will do the exact same if they come to your website and find that there's no new content to read. In fact, they'll see that you haven't published anything in a while, and head on over to Reddit to look at cat memes. If you don't publish any new content for long enough, they'll stop checking your website altogether. First-time visitors will look at your website and see that you haven't published in a couple of months and assume you have abandoned the project to move on to something else. Web users are smart enough to recognize when someone has abandoned their website.

In order to build and maintain an audience, you must regularly publish new content and broadcast it to all of your media channels (Facebook, Twitter, YouTube, etc.). Building a business that regularly publishes great content over a long period of time does not happen by accident. Successful internet business owners do not just publish a new article whenever they are inspired or whenever they feel like it. They know that they need to regularly publish content over a long period of time in order to attract and maintain a following. They create processes and schedules to ensure they are regularly delivering new content to their website, their email list, and their social media platforms.

This chapter is all about choosing the right publishing channels for your business, and building schedules and processes so there's always something new on your website for readers to consume.

In this chapter, you will learn:

- Why consistently publishing new content is critical to your success.

- How to choose which media channels are right for your business.

- Whether or not you should launch a podcast or a YouTube channel.

- Which social networks you should use to promote your business.

- How to develop and stick to a content schedule.

- How to optimize your content for search engines.

- How to identify what to write about when you're out of ideas.

Choose Your Media Channels

When developing your content strategy, your first task will be to determine what platforms you want to publish content on. Your website will serve as the hub for all the content that you produce for your business. But you should also publish content on other platforms, such as Facebook, YouTube, and Twitter. The goal will always be to drive users back to your website so that they can read your content, sign up for your email list, click on your ads, and purchase products that you sell. Your website is where you will make your money, but you can't focus on your website alone, because you won't be able to build an audience without also publishing content on other platforms. You need to leverage other marketing channels so people will come to your website, click on your ads, and buy your products.

Here are some examples of different platforms you can publish content on:

- ACX (audiobooks)

- CreateSpace (paperback books)

- Facebook

- Flickr

- Google+

- Google News (News stories)

- Instagram

- iTunes (Podcasts)

- Kindle (eBooks)
- LinkedIn
- Medium
- Periscope
- Pinterest
- Snapchat
- Stitcher (Podcasts)
- StockTwits
- Tagged
- Tumblr
- Twitter
- Vine
- YouTube

Not every publishing platform will be right for every business. Not everyone should try to run a YouTube channel, have a major presence on LinkedIn, launch a podcast, or rely heavily on Facebook. Focus on the publishing channels that cater to your target audience. At MarketBeat, we only focus on social networks that cater to investors. Publishing content through Facebook, Instagram, and Snapchat won't move the needle for our business because people don't look for investing content on those platforms. However, Twitter, LinkedIn, and StockTwits are excellent publishing channels for MarketBeat content, because there are users actively searching for investing content on those platforms. Identify what social media channels your audience is already using, and focus exclusively on those platforms.

One way to determine what social media platforms your audience is using is to look at what your competitors are doing. If all of your competitors are active on Pinterest, you should probably be leveraging Pinterest as well. If all of your competitors have an active YouTube channel, it's probably working for them as a good source of web traffic. The best way to determine which social media platforms are working for your competitors is by using SimilarWeb (www.similarweb.com). Enter your competitors' websites into SimilarWeb and it will show you which social media channels are referring the most traffic to their websites. SimilarWeb does charge a fee for some of its services, but the basic social media referral information you are looking for is available for free without a login.

There are dozens of different platforms you could publish content on, but not all of them will be worth the effort and you don't have enough hours in the day to properly leverage every available social media platform. The 80/20 rule is in full effect when choosing your publishing platforms—the vast majority of the results that you get will come from the few platforms that are most relevant to your niche. Focus only on the two or three publishing platforms that will generate the best results for your business, and set aside everything else. You will get better traction on the platforms you focus on and still have time to work on your website and build your email list.

At this point, you may not know what social media services and other publishing channels you should focus on. The next several sections of this chapter provide an overview of some major publishing platforms, and will help to determine whether or not each platform is a good fit for your business.

Consider Starting a YouTube Channel

YouTube is the second largest search engine on the internet, after Google. YouTube already has a massive built-in audience, and you can tap into that audience by building a YouTube channel and regularly publishing new videos. This will help you reach new visitors that otherwise would never find your platform. YouTube's recommended videos on its sidebar make it a great platform for discoverability. If you optimize your videos well, new viewers naturally find your content. If they like your content enough, they'll subscribe to your channel and become one of your followers. The mechanics of building out a YouTube channel are beyond the scope of this book, but YouTube has a section called Creator Academy (www.youtube.com/creatoracademy) that will help you get started. There are also several good online courses on Udemy (www.udemy.com) that teach how to do YouTube marketing.

Consider Launching a Podcast

Launching an audio podcast helps turn casual followers into devoted fans. Podcasting is a very intimate media channel. It's almost like your listeners are having a private conversation with you through their earbuds every week. Your followers will feel like they have developed a personal relationship with you by listening to your podcast, even though you may have never met them.

I have been listening to the TropicalMBA podcast (www.tropicalmba.com) since it first launched in 2009, when it was the Lifestyle Business Podcast. I have only met the hosts, Dan Andrews and Ian Schoen, once at a conference, and we traded emails back and forth a few times; but I feel like they're old friends, and we have been having coffee together every week since I first started listening.

Like YouTube, podcasting also has some discoverability benefits. Many people listen to podcasts by subscribing to them on iTunes or Stitcher, both of which have directory features and search engines that allow people to discover new podcasts on the topics that interest them. If you optimize your iTunes and Stitcher listings well, your podcast might show up when someone searches for podcasts about your niche. Podcasting allows potential fans to find out about you and get hooked on your content, without first having to go to your website.

Running a podcast is not a media channel for the lazy. Recording a podcast episode is only a fraction of the work involved with publishing a podcast. You have to prepare for each episode and think of what you'd like to talk about. If you want to have guests on your show, you have to invite them. You have to create a blog post to go along with each new episode. The hardest part of running a podcast is editing. Each episode requires listening to several hours of your own voice and making edits to your recording. Podcasting can be a very rewarding media channel, but it's also a lot of work.

If you would like to launch your own podcast, I recommend signing up for Cliff Ravenscraft's Podcasting A to Z course (www.podcastanswerman.com/atoz). Cliff Ravenscraft has been the go-to expert on podcasting for years, and there's no better place to start. His course teaches you how to develop the format of your podcast, set up WordPress to host a podcast, get the right recording equipment, publish your podcast on iTunes and other platforms, and finally, how to market your podcast. Podcasting A to Z is probably the definitive resource on launching a podcast, but it's not a cheap proposition to take his course at $1,999. If you can't afford that, you should still subscribe to his podcast because he publishes a lot of great podcasting material for free.

Build Your Brand on Facebook and Twitter

Every business should have a presence on Facebook and Twitter because they are currently the two most broadly-used social media platforms. A study from the Pew Research Center showed that 72 percent of all online American adults use Facebook (http://www.pewinternet.org/2015/08/19/the-demographics-of-social-media-users). According to the study, 82 percent of online adults ages 18 to 29 use Facebook, along with 79 percent of those ages 30 to 49, 64 percent of those ages 50 to 64, and 48 percent of those 65 and older. Twitter's usage pales in comparison to Facebook, with only 20 percent of online American adults using their platform, but that doesn't mean you should write it off.

Twitter is a strong platform for organic discoverability, meaning that Twitter users will naturally be able to find your content through features like hashtags, retweets, and suggested accounts to follow. Both Facebook and Twitter are essential tools to engage with your audience and grow your base of followers.

Harness The Power of Twitter

Facebook and Twitter are very different animals. Think of Twitter as an ongoing conversation between you, your followers, and people who might become your followers. Don't just automatically post new articles from your website on your Twitter account and call it good. Regularly engage with the people that follow you by actively starting conversations with them and responding when someone tags you in a Tweet. Also, create content specifically for Twitter, such as short quotes and graphics, and add hashtags appropriately. By creating unique Twitter-only content, you are giving your readers an extra incentive to follow you there, because they won't be getting 100 percent of your content unless they read your tweets.

If you want to build your Twitter following, there is an incredibly powerful tool called SocialQuant (www.socialquant. net) that you should consider using. SocialQuant automatically follows people that tweet with hashtags that are relevant to your business. The idea is that the users you follow will check out your profile and will follow you back if they like the type of content that you produce.

While Twitter isn't a huge focus for me personally, I have

been able to use SocialQuant to grow my Twitter account from 2,500 followers to about 5,500 followers in about 60 days. SocialQuant offers a 14-day free trial and costs $25.00 per month after that.

Facebook Pages, Groups, and Your Personal Profile

There are many different ways that you can use Facebook to grow your audience. You can promote your content on your personal profile, create a Facebook page, create a Facebook group for your audience, or use their advertising platform.

Creating a Facebook page is the default way to promote your business on Facebook, but pages aren't very effective marketing tools anymore. Only a small percentage of people that like your page will actually see your content in their news feed. If you want the majority of your audience to see your content, you have to utilize Facebook's advertising platform and pay to have your posts reach them. In my experience, growing a following for your Facebook fan page is rarely worth the effort. Even if you were to get 10,000 likes on your fan page, it wouldn't matter because Facebook won't show your content unless you pay for the privilege of reaching them through a boosted post. Often not even then.

While it's probably not worth it to put a bunch of energy into building out a Facebook page, creating Facebook groups and leveraging your personal Facebook profile can be incredibly effective ways to build an audience and drive people to your website.

To effectively use your personal profile, try to become Facebook friends with everyone that you have met in person and anyone else that knows who you are. Facebook allows you to have up to 5,000 friends on your personal profile. As long as you don't mind seeing updates from 5,000 people, go ahead and start liberally adding casual acquaintances on Facebook using the "People You May Know" feature. Make it a habit to send five to ten friend requests per day until you reach about 4,500 friends. I wouldn't go much beyond that, because you have to unfriend someone to add a new friend after you've reached the 5,000-friend limit.

Whenever you publish a new article on your website, release a new podcast episode, publish a new YouTube video, or create some of other piece of content, share that content to your Facebook profile. Make sure to format your content specifically for Facebook—liberally use images, tag people in your posts, use hashtags, and add a location to your posts (if it's relevant to do so). There's a good chance that most of your friends who use Facebook in the 24-hour period after your share goes live will see the content you share. Limit yourself to posting something about your blog once every other day so that you don't annoy the friends who aren't interested in your business or niche.

Facebook groups have also become an incredibly powerful marketing tool for entrepreneurs that have any kind of platform. Unlike Facebook pages, members of your Facebook group will actually receive notifications about new content posted to your group page. The "out of sight, out of mind" rule applies, especially on Facebook. If your audience doesn't naturally see your content, they aren't going to go searching for it on your page. The simple fact that Facebook group members will receive notifications for content posted to groups they are a part of, not just news feed items, makes them a more powerful marketing tool than Facebook pages.

Facebook groups also provide a place for your community to discuss your content and share ideas. As you might have noticed, not very many people leave comments on blogs anymore. The conversation has moved over to social media, so it makes sense to provide a natural channel for people to discuss your content on Facebook. Because almost everyone is on Facebook, and Facebook now has nested discussion threads, Facebook groups are a perfect place for audience to talk about your ideas and your content.

One example of a Facebook group that has been put together quite well is Steve Scott's "Authority Self-Publishing" group, which has more than 5,000 group members. Self-published authors use the group as a place to solicit feedback from other authors, get help with their books, and discuss the content that Steve Scott and his partners produce on his website, Authority-Pub (www.authority.pub). This group works particularly well because members are actively engaged and there's a healthy mix of content made by Steve Scott *and* the members of his group.

Consider Using Pinterest, Instagram, LinkedIn, and Snapchat

There are a number of second-tier social media platforms that can be incredibly powerful if they are relevant to your audience. These are platforms like Instagram, LinkedIn, Medium, Periscope, Pinterest, Snapchat, and StockTwits. They may not command the size of audience that Facebook does, but they might be more powerful marketing channels than Facebook– if your audience is active on the platform.

For example, both Pinterest and Instagram are visual platforms that place a heavy emphasis on images. If you create content about cooking or fashion you will want to leverage these platforms, because they are perfectly suited to the type of content you create, and your audience is already on those platforms.

Leveraging second-tier social media platforms is beyond the scope of this book, but there are a ton of great resources available online to learn each of these platforms. Whenever I am looking to learn a new platform, I try to figure out who the two or three leading experts are on that platform. I will then buy their books, subscribe to their podcasts, and listen to all the episodes with a notebook. I'll also buy their online courses and watch all of the videos. When I wanted to learn about publishing books through Amazon, I immediately started reading Steve Scott's (www.authority.pub) content, purchased his online course, and listened to all of the back episodes of his podcast. I also read several ebooks about Kindle publishing from other authors to get a variety of perspectives. By ingesting all of the content produced by Steve Scott and other Kindle publishing experts, I was able to learn most of what I needed to know to publish books through Amazon. I invested one hour per day into learning this topic for about a month to get through the various books, podcast episodes, and online courses produced by the top experts.

Develop Your Content Schedule

When you have decided which publishing channels you want to use in your business, the next step is creating a content schedule, sometimes called a content or editorial calendar. A content schedule is simply a plan for what kind of content you want to publish, and when you want to publish it.

You already know that keeping a consistent publishing schedule will be one of the keys to your long-term success, and your content schedule will ensure that you are regularly publishing content to your website and your other publishing platforms. With a good content schedule in place, you will never forget to write a blog post, publish a podcast episode, or keep your Twitter account up to date.

Here's how to create a content schedule:

- **Step 1: Print Out a Monthly Calendar** – You will be creating a new content schedule for each month. A few days before the end of a month, begin working on the content schedule for the following month. In my experience, the best way to lay out a monthly content schedule is with an old-fashioned paper calendar. A paper calendar provides a visually intuitive way to look at your publishing schedule for an entire month on a single piece of paper. You can either buy a printed calendar at a store, or print one off the internet. I personally print off free calendar templates from WinCalendar (www.wincalendar.com). If you want to go all digital, you can fill out a Microsoft Word calendar template from WinCalendar or put your content schedule directly into Google Calendar.

- **Step 2: Make a List of Your Publishing Channels** – Write out a list of all of the publishing channels that you want to regularly post content out to. This will include your website, your email list, your personal Facebook account, and your Twitter account. This list will also encompass other social networks, your podcast (if you publish one), your YouTube channel (if you create one), and any other places that you plan on regularly publishing content related to your niche. Facebook is a special case. Your personal profile, your business Facebook page, and your Facebook group (if you create one) should each be listed as individual publishing channels.

- **Step 3: Determine Your Publishing Frequency for Each Channel** – For each publishing channel, choose how often you want to publish new content. You might post to some channels, like your Facebook and Twitter account, every day. You may even post to your Twitter account multiple times per day. You may publish to your website once or twice per week. For more involved channels—like podcasting and YouTube— you may only publish once per week or once every other week. Choose a sustainable frequency for each channel and commit to sticking with the publishing cycle that you set.

- **Step 4: Create a Process for Each Channel** – For each publishing channel you plan on utilizing, write out a standardized list of steps that you will complete whenever you create a new piece of content. For publishing a blog post, your steps might include brainstorming, outlining, writing, editing, proofreading, scheduling to WordPress, optimizing for SEO, adding an image, posting your article, and sharing it on your social media channels. Having a standardized process for each publishing channel will speed up the process and make sure that you don't miss any important steps. You will also eventually be able to hand off some of these steps to contractors or employees so that you can put more of your focus on creative tasks. Whenever I write a new blog post, I hand it off to my employee, Rebecca. She will edit the post, proofread it, find an appropriate stock photo, schedule it in WordPress, assign appropriate tags and categories, and schedule it to be published the following week.

- **Step 5: Write Out Your Publishing Schedule** – Take out your paper calendar and start penciling in dates to publish content for each of your channels. The dates that you select should align with the publishing frequency you selected for each channel. For example, if you want to post a new article on your website twice per week, you might write in "Post New Article on Website" in your calendar on every Tuesday and Thursday. Try to be consistent about the days of the week that you post each type of content. Your audience will then get in a habit of checking your website and your other channels for new content on specific days. Publish your most important content on weekdays, because people generally spend less time online during the weekend. Choose dates to publish content for each of your publishing channels according to your publishing frequency until you have done so for all of your channels.

- **Step 6: Set Aside Content Creation Days and Pre-Schedule Content** – Using your calendar, you may plan on publishing some form of content every day of the week. This does not mean that you should be creating content seven days per week. It's much more effective to create content in batches than to try to create content every day. Set aside one day of the week to create all of the content you want to publish for the following week. Write the articles you plan on publishing, and pre-schedule them to post with WordPress. Write the tweets and Facebook posts you want to publish and schedule them with a tool like Buffer (www.buffer.com). Record your YouTube videos, record podcast episodes, and create any other content you plan on publishing in the following week on your content creation day and schedule them to go live according to your calendar. By creating your content in batches and pre-scheduling your content, you will never miss a publishing date, and you will have more free time to work on other parts of your business.

Optimize Your Content for Search Engines

As part of the publishing process that you create for each of your publishing channels, be mindful of the discoverability features that each platform affords you. Search engines are one of the biggest platforms available to your website. Take the time to optimize each of your articles for keyword searches that people might use to find your writing by using the recommendations from the Yoast WordPress SEO plugin (https://wordpress.org/plugins/wordpress-seo). This will ensure that each article has the basic optimizations needed to give your content a fighting chance of ranking in Google search results pages.

Of course, you can go as far down the rabbit hole of learning about search engine optimization as you want to. There are untold numbers of books, podcasts, blogs, and online courses that focus on teaching search engine optimization (SEO). While it's worthwhile to do some basic optimizations on your content, I personally wouldn't focus too heavily on SEO.

As I mentioned previously, you can't rely on Google to send your website search traffic because their business interests aren't aligned with yours. Plus, an algorithm update could change everything. Focus on receiving web traffic from a wide variety of sources so that you are not overly dependent on a single publishing platform.

We often primarily think of SEO in terms of ranking content in Google, but you can also benefit by optimizing your content for discoverability on other platforms. If you have a podcast, you can optimize your iTunes listing and ask your audience for reviews, either verbally on your podcast or by emailing them. Reviews will increase the visibility of your podcast listing in iTunes. If you have YouTube, you can optimize the title, description, and metadata for each video so that your videos are more likely to show up in YouTube. If you write books, you can optimize your listings to get greater visibility on Amazon. You can use hashtags on Twitter and tag people in your posts on Facebook to give your social media updates an extra push. Whenever you create a new piece of content, consider what you can do to optimize it and extend its reach on each of your publishing platforms.

How to Identify What to Write About

When you commit to creating content on an ongoing basis, one of the biggest challenges you will face on a week-to-week basis is figuring out what to write about. You may feel like you have covered all of the important aspects of your niche after writing for several months. You may not be sure what your audience wants to read about, or may not be inspired to write on any particular subject. Fortunately, choosing content topics does not have to be an excruciating process.

Here are some strategies that will help you quickly identify topics to write about:

- **Ask Your Audience** – Send a message to your email list asking your audience what they want to learn about, relating to your niche. If you hear a suggestion more than once, you should probably create a piece of content around the idea that was suggested. For every one person that suggests a topic for you to write about, there are probably 10 or 100 more that want to learn about the same topic, but didn't email you. If you don't have an email list yet, you can use the same strategy using your social media accounts.

- **Cover the Basics** – Every niche has a list of basic topics that everyone interested in that niche needs to learn about. Make a list of 10 to 20 topics that, when read together, will provide a basic level of understanding to anyone who is just learning about your niche. You can also combine these posts together into a PDF document and use it as a lead magnet to collect email addresses.

- **Check What Questions People Are Asking on Quora** – Quora (www.quora.com) is a community-driven question-and-answers website, where anyone can ask a question of other Quora members. Quora is particularly useful for content creation because you can look at the questions people are asking related to your niche. If you see common themes in the questions, you can write an article that addresses those themes. You can also put an abbreviated version of your thoughts on the issue as a response to the relevant questions on Quora, and provide a link back to your article as a way of generating traffic for your website.

- **Review What Your Competitors Are Writing About** – Review the content created by other people in your niche. Arc there any topics they are covering that you have not covered yet? You should never copy a competitor's articles point-by-point, but you can use the subjects that others in your niche write about for inspiration on content that you create. Have any of your competitors written anything that you disagree with, for which you can create a response? You might be able to attract the attention of your competitor's audience if you provide a counterpoint to their ideas.

- **Look for Books in Your Niche on Amazon** – There are more than 2 million ebooks published on Amazon, so there's a pretty good chance at least one book has been written about your niche. Download some of the best-selling books in your niche. Review the table of contents for each book and you may find a subject that you want to write about.

- **Review Forums and Community Sites in Your Niche** – If there are any public discussion forums or community-driven websites in your niche, review them thoroughly. Look for topics that come up repeatedly as they are likely of interest to many readers. Also look for problems that your industry or niche faces to see if you can create content that addresses those problems. Make sure to bookmark any discussion forums in your niche and check back regularly to see what new content users are posting.

- **Look for Industry Events and Conferences** – If there are any big conferences or events for your niche, review the agenda and speaker topics. If you are able to attend, or watch it online, a summary of some of the speakers' talks may make for compelling content on your own website. If you aren't able to participate in the event, the list of topics presented may inspire you to create your own content in some of the same areas.

- **Talk to People in Your Niche** – If all else fails, you can always find people that are interested in your niche, and talk to them directly. Ask them what they want to learn about. Ask them what problems they face in your niche. Ask them what resources they have already found valuable. Ask them what they would like to accomplish. Repeat this process as many times as you can, and look for common themes in the feedback you receive. This will help you determine what topics are interesting to your audience as a whole.

Don't Get Discouraged

You may create content for several months in a row without getting much traction. You might be disappointed with your web traffic, wish you had a bigger email list, or just wish there was more user engagement with your content. You may feel like the only person reading your website is your mom for the first several months of running your business. Don't get discouraged when you find out building an audience takes longer than you thought.

In the first year of running my business, which was originally named American Consumer News, my website never hit more than 10,000 page views per month. By the third year, we would be lucky to get 50,000 page views each month. That same year year, we barely had any email sign-ups and revenue never topped more than a few thousand dollars each month. It wasn't until mid-2010—a *full four years* into my business—that we began getting any real traction. By learning a few industry-specific marketing strategies and developing a scalable publishing model, we were able to grow from less than 100,000 page views per month to more than 1 million page views per month, in a period of just six months.

While it's easy to look at MarketBeat and call it an overnight success, it took four years to figure out a business model that would actually work for our company—and another five years after that to build it into a business that generates seven figures in annual revenue. Overnight successes rarely happen overnight. If you can put your head down, stay focused, and regularly try new content marketing and monetization strategies, you too can be an "overnight success" a few years down the line.

Action Steps

- Choose which social media networks and other publishing channels you will use for your business.

- Sign up for accounts with the services that you plan on using as publishing channels.

- Create your first content schedule.

- Make a list of 20 to 30 topics that you can create content about on your website.

CHAPTER FIVE
Additional Marketing Strategies

IF YOU FOLLOW THE authority publishing business model outlined in this book, creating and marketing great content through your website and your other publishing channels will always be the core marketing strategy of your business.

However, there are several additional marketing strategies that don't explicitly fall under the umbrella of content marketing which you should consider implementing in your authority publishing business. This chapter outlines several of those marketing strategies and techniques you can use to build your audience to make them sticky, so they continue to read your content, click on your ads, and buy your products.

In this chapter, you will learn:

- How to use email marketing to generate sales and keep readers coming back for more.

- How to guest post on other people's blogs to leverage their audiences.

- How to conduct a podcast tour to build your audience.

- How to use paid advertising to grow your business.

- How to identify and copy your competitors' best marketing channels.

Growing Your Email List

Your audience is your business. Without your audience, you just have a website that nobody visits. Your audience is the group of people that will engage with your content, serve as ambassadors for your brand, buy products and services that you sell, and click the ads on your website. In order to turn your casual followers into devoted fans who will consume everything you make, you need a way to communicate with them regularly so that you can send them new content, let them know about what you are up to, and promote the products and services you produce. The best way to do that is through building your email list. While email marketing is a topic that is too broad to cover in its entirety in this chapter, I will attempt to cover the basics and summarize the most important aspects of email marketing in the following sections.

Collecting Email Opt-Ins on Your Website

From day one, begin collecting email opt-ins on your website. You don't need to have your entire email strategy figured out, but you should start collecting opt-ins right away.

In order to get started, you need an account set up with an email service provider like MailChimp (www.mailchimp.com),

Aweber (www.aweber.com), or Drip (www.getadrip.com). You then need an opt-in form plugin on your website, like Opt-in Monster (www.optinmonster.com), Hello Bar (www.hellobar. com), or Popup Domination (www.popupdomination.com). These plugins will integrate with your email service provider account and place the actual opt-in form on your website. When someone completes the opt-in form on your website, they will automatically be added to the email list that is maintained by your email service provider.

In order to convert website visitors into email subscribers, offer something compelling that your readers will want to receive, in exchange for giving you their email address. In the industry, this is known as a "lead magnet". Create something like a free report, video course, or how-to guide that readers will get as a bonus for signing up for your mailing list. As your website becomes more popular, experiment with different lead magnets to see if one lead magnet will work better than another. You can also experiment with the language, or copy, that you use to communicate what readers will receive for signing up for your mailing list. You can view the types of lead magnets and opt-in forms I use in my businesses by visiting www.usgolftv.com and www. MarketBeat.com.

It might be tempting to keep your opt-in forms to a minimum and make them as unobtrusive as possible. You might not want to run a pop-up opt-in form on your website because you personally think they are annoying. Don't let these hang-ups stop you from placing good opt-in forms on your website. Remember that you are building an email list and creating content because you think you can genuinely offer good information and help people in your niche. By making your email opt-ins hard to find, you are doing a disservice to your audience, because you are making it harder for them to subscribe to your content and learn more about your niche.

Your email list will be one of the most important parts of your business, and you have to be aggressive with your opt-in forms if you want to build a sizable email list. Use a pop-up opt-in form, an opt-in form below each post, and an opt-in form in your sidebar to get the most opt-ins.

Crafting Your Email Marketing Strategy

Once your website is up and running, and you have begun to collect email sign-ups, you will want to email your subscribers.

You can start with an autoresponder series that automatically sends new subscribers a series of pre-written emails over time. Since everyone that signs up for your email list will otherwise receive the same emails at the same time, an autoresponder series is the perfect tool to familiarize subscribers with you, share your best content with them, and let them know about your products and services. There's no perfect number of emails or frequency of delivery, but as a general rule of thumb I like to send an autoresponder email once every three days, and include between 15 to 25 emails in my autoresponder series.

Since your autoresponder series will only last between two and three months, you will also want to send broadcast emails, which are messages that are sent to your entire mailing list at one time. Broadcast emails will help keep subscribers that have completed your autoresponder series engaged with your content and your mailing list.

Just as you created a content schedule for your website and publishing platforms, create a calendar for your email list. Send a message to your email list at least once per week to keep them active and engaged with your emails. If you don't send an email for several weeks, people will forget that they subscribed to your email list and will think that you are spamming them. Use your broadcast emails to highlight new content, keep your audience informed about what's going on in your business, sell your products, and promote other people's products as an affiliate.

Writing Emails That Inspire People to Take Action

When you write your email messages, always use your personal name as the "from name" rather than the name of your business. Emails from individuals are more likely to be opened than those from businesses.

Use intriguing subject lines like "Bad News" and "Strange Question?" that will entice readers to open your messages.

Each email should be about a single subject and contain a single call-to-action. When multiple calls-to-action are placed inside a single email, users then have to make an additional decision about which of the actions they want to take. Since there's more of a decision-making process involved in taking action on an email with multiple calls-to-action, subscribers are more likely to make no decision at all, or set the message aside for later.

Use the acronym AIDA to plan out each email sent to your mailing list. AIDA stands for:

- **A**ttention
- **I**nterest
- **D**esire
- **A**ction

Crafting your email to inspire AIDA is an extremely effective strategy to use whenever you want your subscribers to take action.

At the top of your email, you should try to capture your reader's *attention* with an interesting fact or a compelling story. Then, transition into getting the readers *interested* in the product, service, or piece of content you are emailing about. Explain the features and benefits of whatever you are promoting, and show your subscribers how it can help them. The next step is to instill an emotional *desire* in your subscribers. How would they feel if they were to take action on your email? What would their life be like if they said yes to your product or service? The final step is the call-to-*action*. This often comes in the form of a hyperlink to an article, a landing page, or a sales page. The copy for your call-to-action could be as simple as: "Click Here to Get Your Copy of My Cool New Product (Save $100.00!)".

Learn More About Email Marketing

I've written an entire book about leveraging email marketing in your business, titled *Email Marketing Demystified*. In that book, I outline everything that you need to know to maximize the power of email in your business. *Email Marketing Demystified* covers choosing an email service provider, collecting opt-ins, writing great email copy, planning what kind of email to send and how often to send it, generating revenue from your email list, and making sure that the messages you send stay out of the spam folder. You can grab a copy of *Email Marketing Demystified* on Amazon for $2.99 by heading over to www.myemailmarketingbook.com.

Do a Podcast Tour

A creative way to promote your brand and leverage other people's audiences is by getting yourself booked on podcasts that are relevant to your niche. A great time to do this is whenever you have a new product, a new service, or a major piece of content to share. Many authors will do this when they publish a new book as a digital book tour of sorts. When you are interviewed on a podcast, the host is effectively introducing you to their audience and giving you an opportunity to sell your brand to their audience. If you interview well, those who heard your interview may start following your content and become part of your audience. Depending on the relationship you have with the podcast host, you may even be able to directly promote your products on their show, if you give them an affiliate commission for each sale that you make. If that's not an option, it's still worthwhile to be a guest on other people's podcasts, and get your name (and brand) out in front of the right people.

In order to do this, create a list of relevant podcasts where you might be a good fit. Make sure each podcast on the list actually has guests on their shows, because you'll be wasting your time trying to pitch an interview to shows that don't do them. For each podcast on the list, send an email directly to the host inquiring whether or not you would be a good fit for their show. In your email, focus exclusively on the informational value that you can provide to their audience. Never talk about how being a guest may benefit you, because frankly, they won't care. You may not receive a response to your first email, but be persistent. Send a follow-up email every seven days until you get either a "yes" or "no" response from the host.

If a host says yes, prepare for the podcast by reviewing the topics that will be discussed on the show, getting a good microphone, and testing your Skype setup by doing a call with a friend a day before the show using your microphone and headphones. At the end of the interview, the host will probably ask how their listeners can find out more about you. Write out exactly what you want to say to answer this question ahead of time. Focus on your main website and social media profiles. For extra credit, you might offer a lead magnet that is relevant to their audience so that you can collect email addresses.

Booking podcast interviews is a great way to build your audience, but the process of pitching shows can be somewhat time consuming. I recently became aware of a service called Interview Valet (www.interviewvalet.com), which will help get you booked on various podcasts. The service isn't cheap, but it could be a way for you to shortcut the process.

Here is an example of a podcast interview inquiry email that I sent to Jaime Masters of Eventual Millionaire (www.eventual-millionaire.com) during the launch of my first book:

Hi Jaime –

We haven't had an opportunity to interact before, but I hope you enjoyed your trip to Portland for World Domination Summit. Instagram tells me that you kidnapped my good friend, Andy Traub over the weekend. You must have gotten sick of him and let him go because it appears he's made it back to Sioux Falls in one piece (he and I live in the same town).

Anyway, I wanted to email you because I know that you regularly interview millionaires on your podcast (of which I am one). I've built a portfolio of technology-driven businesses that collectively generate seven figures in profit annually (learn more at http://www.mattpaulson.com/about) and have recently finished writing a book titled 40 Rules for Internet Business Success, *which details the strategies and principles that I use to start, build, and grow internet businesses. The book has been endorsed by Dan Miller, John Lee Dumas, and a number of other people. The book is officially launching on 7/21 and I've attached a PDF and Kindle version for your consumption (if you're interested).*

If you think it would be helpful for your audience, I would love to have the opportunity to be a guest on an upcoming episode of your podcast and share some of the lessons that I've learned on my journey.

Let me know if that would be of interest to you.

Have a great day!

Matthew Paulson

Jaime responded positively to my inquiry email and has since had me back on for a second interview. Although I hadn't emailed Jaime directly before sending this inquiry, it worked because she and I have some mutual friends (including a couple that had already endorsed my book).

I also focused primarily on the value I could provide for her audience and used a bit of humor to lighten the tone of the message. I indicated that I was familiar with her podcast by noting that she only has millionaires on her show and by telling her that I met that qualification. All of these things put together indicated to her that I wasn't just someone looking to pitch their stuff, but a friend-of-a-friend that was a fan of her show that could provide value to her audience.

Guest Posting

Writing guest posts for other people's blogs is another effective way to leverage other people's audiences. Just like a podcast tour, you have the direct opportunity to promote your brand to someone else's audience. Writing guest posts for others is a far more scalable strategy than booking podcast interviews, as there are far more blogs and websites than podcasts in most niches.

Any guest post that you write will typically contain one or more links back to your website, which will allow their readers to click back to your website. The back links inside your guest posts may also help improve your search rankings, since one of the primary factors that Google uses to rank websites is whether or not other high quality websites link to them.

When making a list of websites that you might want to pitch a guest post on, be selective and only focus on websites that have some authority and an established audience in your niche. While it's easier to get featured on smaller no-name blogs, it's usually not worth the effort. You would be better served posting the article on your own website than having it featured on a small website that very few people read. Focus on websites that have an audience at least as big as yours.

Also, make sure that the websites you plan on pitching actually feature guest posts somewhat regularly. By focusing only on larger websites that feature guest posts, you will reduce the amount of effort you have to put in to get results.

Guest posting can be an incredibly effective marketing tool, but many people pitch guest posts very ineffectively. Some marketers will use a spray and pray strategy, sending large numbers of impersonal guest post outreach emails to people that they don't know, hoping that someone will respond. They use automated outreach tools to send out hundreds of inquiries at a time. This method is a great way to annoy other website owners at scale, but it probably won't get you very many guest posts.

Effective guest posting is based on relationships. If there's a website that you would like to submit a guest post to, take the time to get know the person running the website. Leave comments on their articles. Follow them on Facebook and Twitter. Sign up for their email list. Engage them on social media.

Find a way to provide them value before you ask for value from them. If they post about a problem or need that they have on social media or their website, find a way to solve their problem for them.

By building a relationship with people you plan on pitching and providing them value, you are more likely to get a positive response from them. After you have been engaging with the person you want to pitch for several weeks, make your request using a carefully-worded email. Focus on the value and the content that you can provide to their audience in your message, and not what they can do for you in your email.

Here is an example of an outreach email that I might send:

Hi [Name] –

It was great to meet you at the Traffic and Conversion Summit in February. Since we first met, I've been following your content about writing through your Twitter account and your email list. Your content has inspired me to up my writing game and I will be publishing a second book this year because you showed me that it's possible.

You do a great job of helping writers create content and publish their books, but I've noticed that there isn't a lot about marketing your book or increasing ebook sales. Since you feature guest posts on your website somewhat regularly, would you be open to allowing me to submit a guest article on your website?

Here are some possibilities for articles that I could write:
- *How to sell ebooks on Barnes and Noble, Kobo, and iBooks with Smashwords*
- *Ten book marketing mistakes made by every first-time author*
- *How to increase sales of your older books by creating a second edition*
- *Five ways to make sure that your Kindle book launch is successful*
- *How to increase book sales by creating an audiobook through ACX*

Let me know if any of these topics might be useful and interesting to your audience. I would love to be able to submit an article and provide some value to your audience as my way of saying thanks for all of the great content that you create.

Thank you!

Matthew Paulson

Publishing guest posts and podcasts are very effective marketing strategies that require nothing but sweat equity. If you're having trouble building an audience, start fielding inquiries to websites, blogs, and podcasts in your industry to see if there is a way that you can get in front of their audience.

Paid Advertising

After your business is more established and you have begun to develop your own products and services, you can experiment with doing paid advertising to grow your email list and sell those products and services. You should not do paid advertising when you are first getting started; if you don't know your numbers, you can lose a lot of money without realizing it.

Once you have developed lead magnets that convert well, have created products that your current subscribers have purchased/enjoyed, have a good understanding of the lifetime value of each of your customers, and know the free-to-paid conversion rate of your email subscribers, you can begin to play with paid advertising. If you start buying ads before you know these numbers, you won't even know if you're getting a return on your investment.

In niche content businesses, paid ads will typically be an offer for some kind of free report or other lead magnet. When a web user clicks through your ad, you will send them to a landing page that offers the user your lead magnet in exchange for their email address. After the user enters their email address and completes your sign-up form, you can show them an offer for one of your paid products on the page that they see after completing your sign-up form.

You can also add them to an email autoresponder series that will send them a mix of content and promotions for your products and services. You should not send people who click on your ads directly to your homepage. Your ads should always send users to a specific page designed to get users to take a single action, such as signing up for your email list.

There are hundreds of companies that offer other companies the ability to create paid advertising campaigns. Every advertising network offers a unique combination of pricing, ad formats, and targeting and tracking abilities. Not all advertising networks are created equal. The performance of individual advertising campaigns will vary dramatically based on the ad networks you choose, the ads that you create, and how you target your ads.

Retargeting Ads

Retargeting is a form of paid advertising that involves showing ads to people who have already visited your website or are already on your email list. You may have visited a website in the past, only to see ads for that same website later that day on another website. This is retargeting in action.

As a paid advertiser, retargeting involves placing a small snippet of code on your website, known as a retargeting pixel, that sets a tracking cookie in the browsers of people that visit your website. Retargeting pixels and their associated tracking cookies allow you to keep track of people that have visited your website and show ads to them specifically.

Retargeting campaigns tend to be a very effective way to promote your email list, your products, and your services because everyone that sees your ads has already been on your website at least once. They are somewhat familiar with your brand. Retargeting campaigns also tend to be inexpensive because the group of people that have visited your website is relatively small compared to any other targeting criteria that you might use.

Retargeting campaigns can be created using both Facebook Ads and Google AdWords, but separate tracking pixels are needed for each ad network. You can also upload your email list to both Facebook ads and Google Adwords to retarget your email subscribers.

Popular Ad Networks

Here are some of the largest ad networks that you might consider using:

- **Facebook Ads** – Facebook Ads (www.facebook.com/ ads) is probably the most powerful ad network for entrepreneurs that run content-driven businesses, because of its advanced targeting abilities. Since Facebook knows a lot of information about its users, you can target users by their specific interests, geographic region, gender, age, relationship status, education, career, and many other criteria. You can also place a Facebook retargeting pixel on your website and target other users who have similar interests and demographics to people that visit your website. Although Facebook has impressive targeting capabilities, it will take some time and experimentation to create a profitable ad campaign, because you won't immediately know which types of people will respond to your ad the best.

- **Google AdWords** – Google AdWords (www.google. com/adwords) is one of the largest advertising networks online. You can use Google AdWords to place ads on Google search results pages and on websites that run Google AdSense ads. The primary way to target relevant users through Google AdWords is based on keywords, but you can also place ads on specific websites, target people that have already been on your website (retargeting), and target people that meet specific demographic criteria. You can use either text-based ads or banner (image) ads using Google AdWords. Google AdWords does tend to be more expensive than some other ad networks, because of the large number of advertisers that compete for ad space.

- **Twitter Ads** – Twitter ads (ads.twitter.com) allow you to build followers on your Twitter account, or have users click through to your website. You can show ads to users that follow specific Twitter accounts, which makes Twitter a very effective tool to reach your competitors' audiences, as you can target users that follow their Twitter accounts. Twitter also allows advertisers to attach lead generation cards to their tweets, which allow users to easily sign up for your email list from directly within Twitter. Twitter's ad network isn't as large or advanced as Facebook Ads or Google AdWords, but it can be very useful in some circumstances.

- **CJ Affiliate** – CJ Affiliate (formerly Commission Junction) (www.cjaffiliate.com) is a large affiliate advertising network that facilities relationships between advertisers and publishers. The primary benefit of running an affiliate advertising program through a network like CJ Affiliate is that you only have to pay publishers when a user takes a specific action, like buying one of your products. Affiliate networks can have a higher barrier-to-entry than some advertising networks, because affiliates may not be interested in promoting new affiliate offers that are untested and unproven. Other affiliate networks include Rakuten Affiliate Network (www.rakuten.com), ShareASale (www.shareasale.com), ClickBank.com (www.clickbank.com) and FlexOffers (www.flexoffers.com).

- **Co-Registration Ad Networks** – Co-registration ads allow you to build your email list by placing an offer on the "thank you" pages that other websites show after someone signs up for their email list or products. The primary benefit of co-registration ads is that you don't have to worry too much about how effective your ad is at getting people to opt in, because you just pay a flat fee per sign-up. You can expect to pay $1.00 to $4.00 per email sign-up that comes through a co-registration advertising network. There is no dominant player in this space, but large co-registration advertising networks include After Offers (www.afteroffers.com), CoregMedia (www.coregmedia.com), Investing Media Solutions (www.investingmediasolutions.com), Opt-Intelligence (www.optingelligence.com) and Tiburon Media (www.tiburonmedia.com).

- **Other Ad Networks** – There are dozens of other ad networks that you might consider testing. Some of them include Infolinks (www.infolinks.com), Media. Net (www.media.net), Revcontent (www.revcontent. com), Bidvertiser (www.bidvertiser.com), Chitika (www.chitika.com), Clicksor (www.clicksor.com), Vibrant Media (www.vibrantmedia.com), BlogAds (www.blogads.com), Amobee (formerly Kontera) (www. amobee.com), and CPX Interactive (www.cpxi.com).

Unfortunately, there is no guaranteed way to determine which advertising networks will work best for your business. You can make some educated guesses about which advertising networks are going to best reach your audience; but ultimately you will need to test different ad networks, targeting strategies, and ad creatives to find ad campaigns that will allow you to profitably acquire customers.

Look to Your Competitors to Identify Marketing Channels

One of the best ways to identify missed marketing opportunities is to study what your competitors are doing. If a competitor of yours is consistently running a Facebook ad campaign or has placed ads on an industry website, you can safely assume that those online marketing channels are working for them, and you should be experimenting with them in your business as well.

Previously, there wasn't a good way to figure out what marketing channels your competitors were using. In the last five years, a number of new tools have come out that mine large quantities of user and advertising data, to provide very revealing information about your competitors' marketing strategies.

My favorite competitive research tool is SimilarWeb (www. similarweb.com), which tracks data from advertising networks, internet service providers, and analytics services to identify useful information about your competitors' websites. SimilarWeb can reveal what keywords users search to find your competitors' websites. It also can show where competitors are spending their online ad dollars, what social networks they use, and what other websites refer people to their website. SimilarWeb also provides demographic details on competitors' customers.

If your competitors are active on Facebook, there are a number of ways to mine their Facebook presence for marketing ideas. You can search for a competitor's Facebook page to see which updates get the most reactions, shares, and comments. You can also see what products, services, offers and discounts your competitors are promoting through Facebook. SumoRank. com provides a free tool that will show the optimal day of the week and time to post on Facebook based on a competitor's engagement data.

If you are trying to outrank your competitors in Google, use tools such as Moz's Open Site Explorer or Majestic SEO to identify why their website might rank better than yours. These tools will show how other websites are linking to your website and your competitor's websites, which is an important factor in how websites get ranked in Google's search results. You can use your competitors' backlinks to identify other websites you might be able to get links from, and send traffic to your website.

Look to Your Audience to Identify Marketing Channels

Another great way to find places to advertise (and other marketing channels) is by talking to people who are part of your audience.

Ask them what resources they use to learn more about your niche. Are there any relevant magazines that they read? What websites do they use to learn more about your niche? Are they part of any specific organizations? What books have they read about your niche? Do they listen to any podcasts in your niche? By figuring out how your audience learns, you might uncover highly-effective paid advertising channels, or free marketing strategies, that you can use to grow your audience.

For example, you might find that almost all of your audience uses the same social network to talk about your niche. You can then become part of that social network, join the conversation, and tactfully promote your company's content, products, and services.

You might find that many members of your audience read the same magazine. If this is the case, you might consider buying an ad to promote your brand in that magazine. The key is to figure out the other media related to your niche that your users are consuming, and use those other channels to promote your brand.

There are two good ways to ask your audience about what other media channels they consume. You can send a survey using Survey Monkey (or another tool) to your email list, and ask them for the information. Make sure to offer some kind of reward to incentivize your audience to actually complete your survey. If you have a smaller email list, you can just ask them to respond directly to the email that you send. Another good strategy is to talk to a few members of your audience on Skype, or over the phone, for a few minutes. You can often glean valuable information through a phone conversation that can get lost in translation over email or an online survey.

Additional Web Marketing Resources

This book provides an overview of a variety of different marketing strategies that you can use to send people to your website, including content marketing, social media marketing, email marketing, podcast tours, guest posting, paid advertising, and retargeting. Entire companies, books, and websites have been created to provide content around each of these marketing strategies. Whenever you begin to implement one in your business, find and reference additional educational resources, so that you can become familiar with the intricacies of each strategy mentioned.

Here are some marketing resources that you might find helpful:

- **Digital Marketer** – Digital Marketer (www. digitalmarketer.com) is a company that offers online training and educational resources that teach marketers and entrepreneurs to drive traffic to their website, increase their conversion rates, and improve social media engagement. They produce online video courses that teach a variety of marketing strategies. Their core product, DM Lab, provides access to a library of training videos for around $40 per month. I have attended one of their conferences (Traffic and Conversion Summit) and found the training material they produce to be very high quality.

- *Traction* **by Gabriel Weinberg and Justin Mares** – Traction is by far the best startup marketing book that I have ever read. The book explores 19 different marketing channels that you can use to grow your customer base, and how to pick which channels are the best fit for your business. The book draws upon the experiences of more than 40 successful startup founders to teach topics like getting targeted media coverage, improving the effectiveness of your email campaigns, improving your search rankings, and finding new marketing channels that your competitors aren't using.

- **Udemy Courses** – Udemy (www.udemy.com) is an online education platform where experts can create online video courses and sell them to the public. There are more than 200 courses on Facebook marketing and more than 30 courses on Google AdWords. If there's a marketing strategy that you want to learn about, there is probably a Udemy course that teaches how to do it. There are some free courses on Udemy, but most of the high-quality courses sell for between $10 and $30.

- **Anything Written by Neil Patel** – Neil Patel, co-founder of CrazyEgg, HelloBar, KissMetrics and QuickSprout, is one of the most knowledgeable people on the planet when it comes to search engine optimization and other online marketing techniques. If you search for highly-competitive keywords like "digital marketing" and "online marketing," his website usually comes up near the top. You can read Patel's blog at www.neilpatel.com/blog and the blog of his current startup, QuickSprout, at www.quicksprout.com/blog.

There are literally thousands of educational resources that teach how to build and market an online business. You might want to consume every bit of educational material you can so as to build the best online business possible, but this is a mistake.

The key is to practice just-in-time learning. Only consume content that is directly related to the marketing strategies that you are working on right now. If you are trying to leverage Facebook to grow your business, take a Facebook marketing course. Don't spend time learning about Twitter, YouTube, or any other marketing channels that you aren't actively pursuing, in this time. You probably won't remember half of the stuff you learned when it comes time to actually market on these channels anyway.

Educational resources can be very helpful when they are directly related to what you are working on right now, but spending too much time learning about entrepreneurship and online marketing can prevent you from actually working on your online business.

Action Steps

- Create a lead magnet and add email opt-in forms to your website.

- Consider using guest posts or a podcast tour to leverage other people's audiences.

- Test paid advertising campaigns after you begin selling your own products and services.

- Review what marketing strategies your competitors are using with tools like SimilarWeb.

- Check out the other marketing resources mentioned in this chapter.

CHAPTER SIX

Making Money with Advertising

THE FIRST FIVE CHAPTERS of this book have focused on getting your website launched, creating great content, and marketing that content so that you can build an audience around your brand. Once these aspects of your business are set into motion, you can begin to generate revenue for your business by leveraging your relationship with your audience to sell them your products and services, and by introducing them to the products and services sold by your advertisers.

When a member of your audience buys something because of your website or your email list, either from you directly or from one of your advertisers, you can make money. You can sell information products or done-for-you services directly to your audience to make money, or you can place ads on your website to generate revenue.

Ultimately, you are in a business that is about creating value. If you can offer educational value to your audience and genuinely help them out, they will reward you.

In this chapter, you will learn:

- Four different ways to make money from your online business.

- How to make money by running display ads on your website.

- How to make money by promoting affiliate offers.

- How to make money with your email list.

- How to find the best combination of ad networks to maximize revenue.

Four Ways to Monetize

There are four basic revenue streams that you can use to generate revenue in your online business:

- **Display Ads** – You can place ad units on your website from advertising networks like Google AdSense, Tribal Fusion, or Media.net. You will earn revenue whenever someone visiting your website views or clicks on an ad. Your advertising network will dynamically select the ads they believe will generate the most revenue, and automatically places them on your website. At the end of each month, the advertising network will calculate your total earnings, take a 30 to 50 percent cut of what you made, and send you the money 30 to

60 days later. You can also sell display ad placements directly to an advertiser.

- **Affiliate Ads** – Affiliate advertising programs pay you a flat fee, or a percentage of a sale, whenever someone purchases a product or completes a lead form after clicking on your affiliate tracking link. You can promote affiliate products through links on your website as well as to your email list. Affiliate programs are often available through affiliate networks like CJ Affiliate and ShareASale. Unlike display ad networks that choose which advertisements to run on your website, with affiliate programs you get to choose exactly which products or services you want to promote. Some affiliate programs, like Amazon Associates, are run independently of an affiliate network.

- **Email Ads** – Wherever there is an audience, there is an opportunity to sell advertising. When your email list grows to 25,000 or 50,000 subscribers, advertisers may be willing to pay to email your list on a CPM (cost per 1,000 impressions) or CPC (cost per click) basis. These ads can be sold directly by you to an advertiser or through an advertising network. You can also promote affiliate ads to your email list by using links and copy that you create, which you have likely seen when your favorite brand shares a relevant product or service from a peer or friend of theirs

- **Product and Service Creation** – Arguably, the best way to make money through your online business is to create your own products and services. When you promote other people's products through advertising, you only keep a small percentage of the revenue generated by your ads. When you promote your own products and services, you keep 100 percent of the revenue generated by the sale (minus any production costs that you have). Creating digital products and services is covered in depth in the next chapter.

These four strategies aren't the only way to make money, but they are the most widely-used, and will be the strategies that you lean on first to generate revenue for your business.

Most content-driven businesses start with revenue sources that are low-hanging fruit, such as display advertisements. You can create an account with an ad network, begin generating revenue in less than 24 hours, and receive your first check around 21 days after the end of your first month (if you use Google AdSense).

As your business grows, you will begin to utilize more advanced revenue generation techniques, like selling ads to be sent to your email list and selling your own information products. While these strategies require much more work, and involve creating direct relationships with advertisers and other partners, they can often be much more lucrative as well. For example, if you were to build an online course that your audience loves, you can create the course once and sell it over and over again to members of your audience for $50 to $250, without doing any additional work for each new customer.

Display Advertisements

As I mentioned, placing display advertisements on your website will almost certainly be how you make your first dollar online. If your website is up and running, you can sign up for an account with Google AdSense or another network, and begin generating money for your business as soon as you can get people to come to your website.

You shouldn't rely exclusively on making money by putting banners on your websites, but they are a nice way to get some early revenue—especially if you can get several thousand people to come to your website each month to read your content and view your ads.

Display advertisements are typically sold through a network, like Tribal Fusion, Media.Net, or Amazon CPM ads. Advertisers will work with the advertising network and create campaigns to promote their products and services. They will bid to place advertisements on webpages that mention certain keywords, to show ads to people that meet their demographic requirements, and to share ads with people who have already visited another website and are being tracked by a retargeting cookie. Whenever someone visits your website, the advertiser will automatically review all of the bids to show ads that will generate the most revenue for the publisher (that's you).

On the publisher side, you will need to first sign up for a publisher account with an advertising network. They will then review your website and make sure that it meets basic quality criteria. After your account has been approved, you will be able to log in to their website and get code snippets that will place banner and text advertisements on your website. The ad units that will be available to you come in standardized sizes as measured by pixel dimensions, such as 300x250, 336x280, 728x90, and 160x600. Commonly, publishers will put a 728x90 banner in their header, a 300x250 banner in the sidebar of their site, and a 336x280 ad inside their content. You can manually place your code snippets inside your theme using widgets or predefined ad spaces in your theme, or you can use one of many WordPress plugins to place them for you.

After you place the ad units on your website, when people start to visit your website and view your ads, you will begin to generate revenue. The advertising network will update your earnings at least once per day, so that you can see how much money you are making by running their ad units. At the end of each month, they will tally up your earnings for the previous month. Typically, you will receive a payment around 30 days after the end of the month, but some networks make payment as soon as 21 days after, while some networks can take as long as 60 days to make payment. Ad networks typically issue payments via ACH, check, or PayPal, but this can vary from network to network.

How much can I earn from display ads?

Your ability to generate revenue by running display ads will depend on four primary factors: what niche you are in, what ad network you choose, how much traffic your website receives, and how well you optimize your ad placements. The price that advertisers will pay largely depends on how many different advertisers are bidding to place ads on your website, and what they are willing to pay. So the average revenue per 1,000 impressions (also known as RPM) can vary dramatically from niche to niche.

Ad prices will be higher in categories where there is a lot of money to be made. Websites about insurance, real estate, investing, and medical malpractice will invariably command higher ad prices than websites about video games, crafting, and gardening. This is simply because advertisers that sell financial products and file lawsuits on people's behalf make a lot more money than businesses that cater to people with relatively inexpensive hobbies.

In less lucrative niches, you may be able to earn $3.00 to $10.00 for every 1,000 people that visit your website. In highly lucrative niches, you can make between $25 and $40 for every 1,000 people that visit your website. You can use the guide outlined in Chapter One to make an estimate of what you can earn per every 1,000 people on your website, based on the keywords that people will use to find your website.

Not all ad networks are equal. Some ad networks will pay dramatically more money for the ad space on your website than others. Large advertising networks, and advertising networks that cater specifically to your industry, will have more advertisers competing to place ads on your website, so they can pay more money to place ads on your website. Conversely, many smaller ad networks have no unique advertisers of their own and simply resell your space to bigger advertising networks and exchanges, like AdX. Focus your efforts on large advertising networks, like Google AdSense and other networks mentioned in this chapter, to make sure that you are on an advertising network that has a healthy level of advertisers competing to place ads.

Since display advertisements are generally sold on a cost per 1,000-impressions (CPM) or a cost per click (CPC) basis, your revenue will go up as more people visit your website. When more people visit your website, more people will view your ads, click on them, and buy products and services from the advertisers.

Choosing a profitable niche, picking the right ad network, and placing optimal ad units on your website won't matter unless you get people to come to your website. In order to grow your revenue to $1,000 per month, and then $10,000 per month, you are going to need to build an audience and get tens of thousands of people to visit your website each month. Fortunately, we we reviewed many methods for doing this in the last chapter.

The other piece to growing your advertising revenue is maximizing the effectiveness of your ad placements. You will want to put them in highly-visible places on your website, And this typically involves placing them "above the fold", meaning that users can see the majority of your ads without having to scroll down in their web browser. When you put ads on the bottom of your website, very few people will see and click on them, which will hinder your ability to generate revenue.

You should also put your ads near the main content on your website, because that's what most readers will be focusing on.

I will generally put a 728x90 horizontal banner in the header of my website, a 300x250 or 336x280 ad unit at the top of my sidebar, and another 300x250 or 336x280 ad unit somewhere inside each post. This combination of ad units tends to generate a relatively high click through rate, without creating a bad viewing experience for your users.

Google AdSense

Google AdSense (www.google.com/adsense) is the 800-pound gorilla in the display advertising world. Google AdSense enables publishers to access inventory from Google's own advertiser network, Google AdWords, and from dozens of other partner networks that tie into Google AdSense. More than 1 million publishers use Google AdSense to generate revenue on their websites, and Google generated more than $67 billion in advertising revenue in 2015 (http://www.statista.com/statistics/266249/advertising-revenue-of-google).

Because of Google's massive network of advertisers, many publishers find that it's more profitable to run Google AdSense ads than ads from any other advertising network. This is not universally true, but AdSense does tend to perform better than other networks in highly competitive categories. It is a great place to start making money on your website through paid advertising.

In order to run Google ads on your website, you will need to apply for a Google AdSense account at www.google.com/adsense. As part of the application process, you will need to provide Google with a link to your website, bank account information so that Google can pay you, and tax information so that Google can file the appropriate tax forms at the end of the year. After your application has been approved, you will be able to log in to Google AdSense and get ad tags that you can place on your website.

When creating your ads, make sure to stick to Google's recommended ad sizes and choose a color scheme that blends in with your website. If your website gets any meaningful amount of traffic, you should begin to see revenue show up in your AdSense account within a day of placing your ad units. Google updates earnings numbers periodically throughout the day, so you will always have a pretty good idea of how much you are making.

At the end of the month, Google will tally up your earnings and, as long as you hit the $100 threshold, they'll issue a payment to you around the 21st of the following month. If you don't happen to hit $100 in earnings for your first month, your earnings will roll over and be added to the next month's earnings. In the United States, Google makes payments via ACH directly into your checking or savings account. Publishers in other countries may have access to additional forms of payment.

Optimizing Google AdSense

Google AdSense continues to be one of my company's largest sources of revenue. Our network of financial news websites attracts between 3 million and 5 million page views per month, and we've found that Google AdSense is an extremely effective way to monetize. I have personally been running Google AdSense ads on my websites for more than 10 years, have done hundreds of experiments, and have tried every combination of ad units and colors. I have learned a lot during those ten years, and discovered several strategies and best practices that every AdSense publisher should be aware of.

Here are my suggested best practices for AdSense publishers:

- **New Publisher? Take the "Optimizing AdSense" Class** – If you're just getting started with Google AdSense, take the time to watch the videos from Google's "Optimizing AdSense" course, located at https://optimizingadsense.withgoogle.com/course. The video course provides a good overview of how AdSense works and how to properly place your ads.

- **Check Out the Opportunities Tab** – Inside your Google AdSense account, there is a tab titled "Optimization" that will give you a list of specific recommendations that you can implement to improve your website's earnings. The opportunities tab might suggest that you place different sizes of ad units on your website or change the colors of your ad to better match your site.

- **Use Recommended Ad Sizes** – Some ad sizes have a lot more advertiser demand than others. Make sure to run ad units that are listed as "recommended" when creating your ads. In my experience, I've found that running a 728x90 ad in the header, a 300x250 ad in the top of the sidebar, and a 336x280 ad inside the content of each post works best, but your mileage may vary depending on your website's layout and your audience's behavior. You can run up to three AdSense units on each page, so make sure to use them all.

- **Place Units above the Fold** – If you want your users to click on an ad, you're going to have to put it where people will actually see it. That means your primary ad(s) should be visible to the user when they first load the page without having to scroll.

- **Show Both Text and Display Ads** – When creating an ad unit, you have the option to only show text ads, to only show display ads, or to show both text and display ads. In order to maximize your earnings, make sure to show both text and display ads on all of your units.

- **Don't Block Ads** – AdSense gives you full control over what ads are shown on your website. I recommend that you don't block any ads in order to maximize revenue, because you may end up blocking high-paying ads from running on your website. The only time you might consider blocking an ad is if it's (A) extremely inappropriate for your audience or (B) a direct competitor is advertising on your site.

- **Regularly Split Test Unit Sizes and Positions** – Your initial ad layout generally won't be the most optimal for your site. I recommend trying out different combinations of ad sizes and positions to see which generates the highest CPM (earnings per 1,000 visitors). ProBlogger has put together a guide that teaches how to create AdSense split tests, which can be accessed at http://www.problogger.net/archives/2008/05/16/how-to-split-test-ab-test-your-adsense-ads.

- **Use "AdSense Experiments" to Test Colors and Fonts** – I recommend regularly experimenting with your top-performing ad units using the "AdSense Experiments" tool. This tool will allow you to easily see if changing colors, fonts or font sizes has a measurable impact on your earnings. Make a series of five or six tests for your best-performing units, and run them one-by-one until your units are well-optimized. Google has put together a guide about using AdSense Experiments, which can be accessed at https://support.google.com/adsense/answer/6321879.

- **Render Your Units with High Click-Through Ratios First** – Not all ads that load on your page will pay the same amount per click. Google will show the highest-available CPC ads on the unit that renders first in your HTML, so you want to make sure that your highest CTR ads are rendering first in the page.

- **Use Link Units for Additional Revenue** – Link units are relatively small units that can be placed in addition to the main three AdSense units on your page. They won't generate a lot of revenue, but can add a nice boost when placed appropriately. You can learn more about link units at https://support.google.com/adsense/answer/15817.

- **Use Google Custom Search as Your Site Search** – Google Custom Search is a nice way to add incremental revenue to your AdSense account. By using Google as your on-site search, you'll receive a share of any ad revenue generated from the search. You can learn more about adding a custom Google Search form to your website at https://developers.google.com/custom-search-ads.

- **Use Ezoic to Find Optimal Ad Units** – Ezoic (www.ezoic.com) is a Google Certified Publishing Partner that offers web-based software and artificial intelligence to find the best possible ad sizes and ad placements on your website. Ezoic will integrate with your existing AdSense account and your website to automatically run experiments to determine which combination and placement of ad units is best for your website.

Other Ad Networks

Of course, Google AdSense is not the only game in town. There are hundreds of other ad networks that you can use in addition to or in place of Google AdSense. None of the other networks have been able to match the earnings generated by Google AdSense on my websites, but your mileage may vary depending on what niche you are in.

Still, I like to use a few other ad networks, in addition to Google AdSense, as a nice way to generate incremental revenue on top of what my websites earn. For example, I might add some additional units from AdBlade, Vibrant Media, and

Amazon CPM ads on my websites, below the content or lower in the sidebar. By adding ad units from these other networks, I can often increase my revenue per page view by between 25 percent and 50 percent.

Here are some other advertising networks that you might consider using on your websites:

- **AdBlade, Taboola, and RevContent** – AdBlade (www.adblade.com), Taboola (www.taboola.com) and RevContent (www.revcontent.com) are three advertising networks that offer sponsored-content advertising units. These are typically large ad units that run below the main content of your post and feature links to articles that can politely be referred to as click bait. Examples of ads that run on these networks include, "20 Times Kate Middleton Showed Off More Than She Should Have!" and "This is the 1 Video Hillary Never Wanted Anyone to See." While these ads are somewhat spammy, many publishers run them because they pay very well. A single ad unit from these networks will often earn you between $1.50 and $3.00 for every 1,000 people that visit your website.

- **Amazon CPM Ads** – Amazon CPM ads (associates. amazon.com) is a relatively new CPM ad network that is run through Amazon's affiliate program, Amazon Associates. As this book is being written, Amazon CPM ads are still in beta and not available to all Amazon Associates affiliates. While this network is relatively new, my early experiments lead me to believe that Amazon CPM ads will be extremely competitive compared to other CPM ad networks. Amazon CPM ads support standard Interactive Advertising Bureau (IAB) ad sizes, such as 728x90, 336x280, and 300x250.

- **BlogAds** – BlogAds (www.blogads.com) is an advertising service that caters specifically to bloggers.

BlogAds is not a traditional advertising network that will automatically rotate ads from a wide swath of advertisers, but rather allows a single advertiser to buy out an ad slot on your website for a fixed fee. These ads can work well if you have an established audience that advertisers want to be able to access, but it may be hard to attract advertiser interest if you're first getting started. BlogAds supports most standard IAB ad sizes.

- **Conversant** – Conversant (formerly ValueClick Media) (www.conversant.com) is an advertising network that runs campaigns for more than 5,000 brands each month. They support all standard IAB ad sizes and also offer a variety of unique formats, including in-text rollovers, rich media ads, and interstitial ad units.

- **Media.net** – Media.net (www.media.net) serves ads from the Yahoo! Bing Contextual Ad Network, which enables publishers to access a large pool of local and national advertisers. Media.net supports all standard IAB ad sizes and has access to demand-side platform (DSP) ad exchanges. Media.net's large pool of advertisers have netted them some big-name publishers, including *Forbes*, *Reuters*, *Cosmopolitan*, and *Esquire*. Media.net also has no minimum traffic level, which makes it accessible to website owners that are first getting started.

- **Exponential** – Exponential (formerly Tribal Fusion) (www.exponential.com) offers some of the highest CPM rates available. They provide a dedicated account manager, offer real-time reporting, and support all standard IAB ad sizes. The only major downside is that Exponential requires publishers to have 500,000 page views per month to get approved for an account.

- **Vibrant Media and Info Links** – Vibrant Media (www.vibrantmedia.com) and Infolinks (www.infolinks.com) are two companies that eschew traditional banner ads and instead generate revenue for publishers by inserting ads that appear when users hover over certain keywords on your website. The main benefit of these networks is that their ad units do not take up a big block of space in your website's design like traditional banner ads do.

The advertising networks listed above are a small sample of additional advertising networks that you can use on your website. There are some other good networks out there, but I have personally used or tried each of the networks listed in this section, so these are the ones I can speak to. On my websites, I always use Google AdSense as my primary ad network and put AdSense ads in the best ad slots on my website. I will place a sponsored content ad from AdBlade or Dianomi (www.dianomi.com) below each post on my sites. I often place CPM ads from Amazon CPM Ads or Tribal Fusion lower in the sidebar or below my AdBlade units. If I want to get more aggressive with ad placements, I will place Vibrant Media's text ads on my website.

Advertising networks tend to come in and out of favor over time, so these recommendations may eventually become dated. MonetizePros maintains a good list of best-performing ad networks on their website, which is updated regularly and can be accessed at http://monetizepros.com/display-advertising/what-are-the-top-ad-networks.

Expect Unsolicited Ad Pitches

Once your website gets several thousand visits per month, you will probably begin to get unsolicited pitches in your email inbox from advertising networks you have never heard of. They will make big promises about how they can generate additional revenue from your website. Most of the time, these ad networks are just reselling your website's ad space to big ad exchanges, and aren't really providing any unique value that any other ad network can't also provide. You can safely ignore these solicitations. If you are using Google AdSense or the other networks above, you are probably already working with better networks than the network that is sending you an unsolicited pitch.

Advanced Display Advertising Monetization Strategies

Here are some more advanced monetization strategies you may use as your business grows:

- **Split Test Ad Placements** – The revenue that you generate by running ads on your website can vary dramatically depending on the size of ad units you use and where you place them. Once you have enough traffic to run statistically-significant experiments, regularly test different sizes and placements of banner ads against your current ad layout to see if you can identify a more optimal ad layout. To perform a valid test, show 50 percent of users your current ad layout and your new test layout to the other 50 percent of users. After a few weeks, check which layout performed better. If your new layout generated more revenue, make that your new default layout.

- **Use Ezoic to Force Google AdSense to Compete with Other Networks** – If you use Google AdSense, you can use Ezoic (www.ezoic.com) to integrate with Google's Ad Exchange, also known as ADX. By using ADX, you can make Google AdSense compete with hundreds of other CPM ad networks for the ad space on your website using ADX's real-time bidding engine. ADX also offers the added benefit of being able to add five ad units per page, compared to the normal limit of three ads per page for Google AdSense. You can learn more about using ADX through Ezoic at http://blog. ezoic.com/adsense-vs-google-ad-exchange.

- **Sell Ads Directly to Advertisers** – You may be able to command a premium rate on your website's ad space if you work directly with your advertisers. Ad networks will take a 30 to 50 percent cut from what you earn. By working directly with advertisers, you can eliminate that fee, and you may be able to command a higher CPM rate if your audience is highly relevant.

- **Use DoubleClick for Publishers to Manage Your Ad Slots** – DoubleClick for Publishers (www.google.com/ dfp), also known as Google DFP, is a comprehensive hosted ad serving platform that streamlines ad management. Google DFP is particularly useful if you sell ads directly to advertisers. Google DFP also allows Google AdSense and Google Ad Exchange to compete against any other ad networks you have that support Google DFP in real-time, so that you can earn the most possible revenue out of each ad impression.

Affiliate Marketing

Affiliate marketing is a type of online advertising that pays publishers and marketers a flat fee or a percentage of a sale when a user takes a specific action.

For example, you might review a product on your website and include an affiliate link to Amazon, so that readers can purchase the product. If one of your readers clicks on your affiliate link and buys that product from Amazon, you will receive a percentage of the revenue that Amazon makes from the sale.

If you run a financial website like I do, you might promote a product like TurboTax, which runs their affiliate program through CJ Affiliate. When I place a banner ad on my website or send an email to my mailing list about TurboTax, and someone purchases a license to the software, I would receive a flat fee commission for generating the sale.

Affiliate Ads vs. Display Ads

When you run display ads on your website, the advertiser takes primary responsibility for the success of their ad placements because they are simply paying for each click or each impression, regardless of whether or not the user buys anything. When you promote products through an advertiser's affiliate program, you only get paid when a member of your audience clicks through and buys something, which creates a shared responsibility between you and the advertiser for success.

You might wonder why you would ever promote an affiliate program if more of the burden to generate results is on your side, but affiliate ads can be very lucrative if you find an affiliate program that is a good fit for your business.

Affiliate ads tend to be much more flexible than display ads in terms of where you place them. You generally can't include display ads in any messages that you send to your email list, but you can include banners and links to promote affiliate programs. You have the flexibility to include affiliate links naturally in your content, just like you would any other hyperlink. If you are going to link to a product anyway, you might as well get an affiliate commission if someone ends up buying it. Of course, you also have the ability to promote affiliate programs through traditional banner ads, like you would with a display advertising network.

Affiliate Networks and Standalone Programs

Affiliate programs can either be run independently through the advertiser's own website or through a network like CJ Affiliate or ShareASale. As a publisher, it won't matter too much whether or not a program is run independently. The only difference will be which website you log in to when you need to get ad copy and, potentially, how you receive payments from the advertiser.

Generally speaking, affiliate programs that run through a network are viewed as being more reputable than standalone programs, as they have likely been vetted by that third-party. However, if you are promoting a well-known advertiser, you shouldn't have any problems getting paid if they're running their affiliate program independently.

In order to find affiliate programs for you to promote, your best bet is to start by creating accounts with some of the larger affiliate networks and using their internal search tools to find advertisers with active affiliate programs. For example, with CJ Affiliate, you can use their search tool to find advertisers with affiliate programs in specific categories, and affiliate programs that cater to specific geographic areas. You can also see how much current publishers are earning on average for each program, which will help you identify what programs may be the most lucrative to promote.

Here are some of the larger affiliate networks and programs:

- Amazon Associates – http://www.associates.amazon.com
- Avangate – http://www.avangate.com
- CJ Affiliate – http://www.cj.com
- ClickBank – http://www.clickbank.com
- eBay Partner Network – http://partnernetwork.ebay.com
- FlexOffers – http://www.flexoffers.com
- Rakuten Affiliate Network – http://marketing.rakuten.com/affiliate-marketing
- ShareASale – http://www.shareasale.com

Rules of the Road for Affiliate Marketing

If you are participating in an affiliate marketing program, be aware that there are certain FTC rules that require you to disclose when you are getting paid to endorse a product, or if you are linking to a product or a service through an affiliate link. You can read the FTC's full guidelines for how to properly disclose affiliate links at http://bit.ly/ftcaffiliate, but the general rule of thumb is that consumers should be easily aware of your affiliate relationship disclosure. You might do something as simple as putting the words (Sponsored Link) next to any affiliate links to avoid running afoul of the FTC .

Beyond the legal requirements of promoting affiliate programs, there are a few other best practices that you should follow when promoting affiliate programs.

First, always be transparent about the fact that you are getting paid to promote a product or service. Nothing will taint your credibility with your readers more than promoting something you are getting paid for and not telling them about it.

Second, only promote products and services that you endorse and would use personally. Never promote products that you wouldn't encourage a close friend to use. It's not hard for readers to figure it out when you are only writing about a product or service because you are getting paid to do so.

Finally, don't let your relationship with an advertiser affect your content. You will gain more credibility with your readers by writing about both the pros and cons of any product you are promoting than you will by only writing about the positive aspects.

How to Promote Affiliate Programs

There are several ways that you can direct your audience to an affiliate advertiser's ads:

- **Product Reviews** – Write a review of the advertiser's product or service, and put it on your website. Write about what the product or service does, along with its features and benefits. Include your personal experience and any perks or downsides to gain additional credibility with your audience. At the end of your review, include a link to buy the product or service, using your affiliate link.

- **Place Affiliate Links in Articles** – Whenever you mention a product or service in an article, consider including an affiliate link to buy that product. For example, whenever I mention a book on my personal website, I will include an affiliate link to buy that book on Amazon. By including these links, my readers are able to easily purchase a copy of the book I recommended, and I will earn a small commission for the sale that was generated from my website. The 80/20 rule applies to this strategy. Don't bother signing up for a bunch of affiliate programs to get commissions for products that you write about once. Sign up for broad programs like Amazon Associates, that allow you to link to thousands of products and sign up for services that you will mention over and over again on your site.

- **Promote Products Through Email** – You can include an email in your autoresponder series that promotes a specific affiliate program. The email should be a mix of an endorsement and a review, that describes what the product or service does and why you use it. At the end of the email, include an affiliate link where your readers can buy the product or service.

- **Place Banner Ads on Your Website** – Just like with display ad networks, most affiliate programs will make banner ads that promote their products and services that you can use on your website. If you are considering giving an affiliate banner ad a prominent placement on your website, make sure to test it against running ad units from Google AdSense and other ad networks. Typically, an affiliate banner ad will not perform as well as Google AdSense or another network, unless the offer is extremely relevant to your audience.

Monetizing Your Email List

Your email list can be an incredibly powerful way to generate revenue from your audience. After you have built a sizable email list, you may find that you make more money by selling ads and promoting your own products to your email list than you earn from the ads on your actual website. There are several ways to monetize your email list, but the four most effective strategies are promoting your own products, promoting other people's products as an affiliate, working with an email advertising agency to send emails to your list on behalf of advertisers, and putting co-registration ads in your email sign-up process.

Whenever you launch a product, you should send a series of emails to your list about your product. Jeff Walker's book, *Launch*, offers great ideas about how to use your email list to promote a product launch. You can also periodically re-launch products or offer discounts to drum up sales for your products.

If you don't have anything to promote, you can find offers on an affiliate network and use the same type of content to promote other people's products in exchange for an affiliate commission on each sale that you generate. You won't have much success promoting products that are outside your niche, but you can do very well when promoting a service that's relevant to your audience, and especially when subscribers get a special discount or bonus for using your link.

Just as you can make money on your website by running display ads for a network like Google AdSense, you can also generate revenue by sending email advertisements to your mailing list on behalf of advertisers. Selling ads against your email list is a great long-term strategy when your list grows in size, but it's difficult to do when you are starting out. Once you get to about 25,000 subscribers, you should start looking at how to find advertisers that might pay to email your mailing list.

It might be far-fetched to think that you will one day have such a large email list, but remember that list growth is cumulative. If you can attract 1,000 new opt-ins every month, you'll have 25,000 subscribers after just two years.

Email advertising is a media that is primarily sold directly to advertisers, and through niche advertising agencies focused on specific industries. There are no big ad networks that will work with just anyone to monetize their email list. You have to establish a relationship with an agency that sells email advertising on behalf of your niche, or make direct deals with advertisers.

While setting up email advertising relationships isn't the easiest thing to do, they can be incredibly lucrative. Some advertisers are willing to pay as much as much as $50 per 1,000 people on your mailing list to send a single email message. If you have a list of 20,000 subscribers, you just made $1,000 by sending a single email.

Co-Registration Advertising

You can also monetize the thank you page that your readers see after they sign up for your mailing list with a co-registration advertising unit. When a user signs up for your mailing list, they will be presented with a list of additional offers that they can also choose to opt in to. If a new subscriber selects any of the offers listed, you'll receive a small commission from the advertiser, and the subscriber's name and email address will automatically be passed on to the advertiser.

The amount of money that you will make from co-registration advertising will vary depending on the niche and the number of people that sign up for your email list every month. For lower-value and general interest mailing lists, you might be able to make an average of $0.15-$0.25 for every new subscriber that sees your co-registration advertising unit. For some specific niches, like finance and investing, publishers make between $0.50 and $1.00 for every subscriber that sees their co-registration advertising unit.

There are a handful of companies that run co-registration ad networks, including After Offers (www.afteroffers.com), CoregMedia (www.coregmedia.com), Investing Media Solutions (www.investingmediasolutions.com), Opt-Intelligence (www.optingelligence.com), and Tiburon Media (www.tiburonmedia.com). I run co-registration units from After Offers and Investing Media Solutions on MarketBeat and on my personal website.

Creative Ways to Monetize Your Business

There are several other creative strategies that you can use to make money in your business that don't fall neatly into the broad categories of display advertising, affiliate marketing, selling products and services, or monetizing your email list.

Here are several additional ways that you can make money through your online business:

- **Publish a Book** – You can take the ideas that you write about on your blog, package them into a book, and sell it on Amazon. While writing a book might sound like an overwhelming task, there are services like Archangel Ink (www.archangelink.com) that will do all of the heavy lifting for you, such as cover design, editing, layout, ebook formatting, etc. in exchange for a small fee. If you don't have time to write a 30,000 to 50,000 word book, you can put together some of your best blog posts, have them professionally edited, and publish them as a standalone book. I recently did this with some of my best blog posts in a book called *Business Growth Day by Day*, which can be accessed at www.businessgrowthdaybyday.com. To learn more about publishing a book on Amazon, I recommend visiting Steve Scott's website, www.authority.pub.

- **Create a Mobile App** – If there's a specific task in your niche that a piece of software can make easier, consider creating a paid iOS or Android app, and promoting it your audience. To learn more about how to develop your own mobile app, read the book *Idea to iPhone: The Essential Guide to Creating your First App for the iPhone and iPad* by Carla White. The book teaches you how to develop your idea, design your app, hire a developer, and make a big splash with your launch.

- **Land Paid Speaking Gigs** – Some entrepreneurs leverage their expert status to land paid speaking gigs at conferences and other events. This strategy can be lucrative when you are well-known in your industry, but it can be a grind when you are first getting started. You may not even get paid for your first several speaking gigs, and you will have to spend numerous hours preparing for each talk that you give. Because of the preparation, skills, and travel required, promoting yourself as a public speaker isn't for everyone. If you have the gift of gab and can put together a good presentation, marketing yourself as a public speaker might be a nice way to generate additional income.

- **License Your Content** – There are a few companies, like ACI Group (www.aci.info), that will license your blog content and sell it for inclusion in large research databases like Lexis Nexis. You won't make a killing from these licensing deals, but if you produce a large amount of content, you could generate a few hundred dollars each month from a licensing deal with a company like ACI Group.

- **Podcast Sponsorships** – If you publish a podcast and gain a sizable audience, there are certain advertisers that may be interested in paying you to read an ad for their product or service on your podcast. You can learn more about getting sponsors for your podcast by checking out podcast advertising networks like Midroll (www.midroll.com) and Archer Avenue (www.archeravenue.com).

Wrap-Up

Experimenting with different ad networks, promoting affiliate programs, selling paid email sends to advertisers, and finding other creative ways to generate revenue are my favorite parts of running an online business.

By finding a better ad network, switching to a more optimal ad layout, or identifying an affiliate program that is a great match for your audience, you can increase your business's monthly revenue for years down the line. If you run a successful split test that increases ad revenue by 5 percent, that means you are making 5 percent more money each month for as long as you run your online business.

Figuring out ways to squeeze more money out of your online business can be a fun and profitable use of your time, but remember that your ad placements and monetization efforts shouldn't come at the expense of the experience your audience has on your website.

If your website is loaded down with ads, or if you send advertising emails to your mailing list every day, you will probably drive away a good portion of your audience. If you put no ads on your website, and never try to sell anything to your audience, you won't ever make any money.

In order to build an online business that lasts, you need to find a balance between your monetization efforts and the experience that you create for your audience.

Action Steps

- Sign up for a publisher account with Google AdSense and at least one other ad network.

- Place your first ad units on your website.

- Sign up for an account with CJ Affiliate or another affiliate network and find two or three affiliate programs that you can promote.

- Write a review of a product or service that you are an affiliate for and post it to your website.

- Consider what strategies you can use to generate income from your email list.

- Think about what creative ways you might be able to generate income from your business.

CHAPTER SEVEN

Making Money with
Digital Products and Services

WHEN YOU PROMOTE OTHER people's products and services on your website through display ads and affiliate offers, you only get to keep a small fraction of the revenue generated. When an advertiser pays to place an ad, they generally expect to earn back a minimum of three times what they pay for their ads in sales. That means that the advertiser who pays $1 to be in your sidebar is making *at least* $3 because of that ad, while you're only making 70 cents from it (after the ad network's fees). I don't know about you, but I'd rather be the one making $3 than the one making 70 cents.

The way that you can capture the full monetary value of your audience is to develop your own products and services that supplement the products and services sold by your advertisers.

When you place ads on your website, you only do marketing work, and capture between 15 percent and 25 percent of the value that you create for your advertisers. When you create your own products and services, you do 100 percent of the work involved with marketing, product design, creation, operations, delivery, and customer support, but you also keep 100 percent of the revenue that you would otherwise be sending to your advertisers. Product creation is a lot more work than simply running ads on your website, but it can also be a lot more lucrative.

I'm not suggesting that placing advertisements on your website or selling your own products and services are mutually exclusive options. Eventually, you will probably run ads on your website *and* sell your own products and services to your customers. Most information-driven businesses are not zero-sum.

Just because a member of your audience buys something from one of your advertisers does not mean that they won't also buy something from you. By selling a mixture of your own products, and promoting the products and services of advertisers, you can earn a healthy income from your own products while maintaining the income diversity that running advertisements on your website affords.

In this chapter, you will learn:

- The most common types of digital products and services that are sold by online businesses.

- Why people will buy digital products from your business.

- When to start launching digital products in your business's life cycle.

- How to create your first digital product.

- How to make sure your product launch is a success.

- Helpful tools to make creating, launching, and selling digital products easier.

What are digital products and services?

In the world of content-driven online businesses, digital products are packaged educational content that teach buyers how to do something. Chris Guillebeau's unconventional guides (www.unconventionalguides.com) are great examples of digital products that are produced and marketed well. Guillebeau made a name for himself by visiting every country in the world over a period of about 11 years. He used the expertise he learned while traveling to produce a number of digital products, including a guide called Upgrade Unlocked (www.upgradeunlocked.com) that teaches readers how to get free airline tickets and hotel bookings by earning rewards points using creative strategies, such as credit card sign-up bonuses.

Guillebeau currently sells nine of these "unconventional guides" that teach readers about business, travel, and personal freedom. Each guide contains a well-produced and well-researched PDF document that is about 100 pages long, along with a number of other pieces of bonus content. They are available at three different price points, that tend to range between $39 and $97, with different features and benefits at each price point. He uses a service called Gumroad (www.gumroad.com) to handle the sale, payment processing, and delivery of his digital products.

There are a variety of different kinds of digital products that online entrepreneurs sell:

- **E-books and PDF Guides** – Ebooks and guides are the most common types of digital products that are sold online. Because they are relatively inexpensive to produce and sell, many online entrepreneurs sell an ebook or a guide as their first digital product. You can usually outline and write an ebook or guide yourself, and sales tools like Gumroad make selling and delivering digital products easy. Ebooks can sell between $0.99 and $9.99 through ebook retailers like Amazon. When you sell ebooks through your own website, and include add-on bonuses, that price point can easily jump to between $19 and $99.

- **Online Courses** – Online courses are the next step up from a PDF Guide. Usually an online course involves recording a series of videos or a PowerPoint presentation that contains the key bullet points. Online courses should teach participants to complete a specific task, such as How To Publish a Book on Amazon Kindle or How To Build a Treehouse in Your Backyard. Prices for broad market courses tend to range between $19 and $99. In some specific niches, such as business training, online courses can sell for much higher price points. As I mentioned before, I once paid $2,000 for an online course, because I knew I would get far more than $2,000 worth of value from that course. Online courses can be sold directly through your website or through one of many online educational platforms, such as SkillShare (www.skillshare.com) or Udemy (www.udemy.com). To view examples of courses that are well put together, I suggest reviewing some of the best-selling courses on Udemy, such as "An Entire MBA in 1 Course," which can be viewed at https://www.udemy.com/an-entire-mba-in-1-courseaward-winning-business-school-prof).

- **Coaching Calls** – People that are your biggest fans will be willing to pay for access to you, whether that be through an individual coaching call or through a group coaching call where you take questions from multiple people over an hour or so. Typically, coaching calls are sold in a package of multiple sessions spread out over several weeks or months. For example, you might sell a 1-hour biweekly coaching call over the course of 12 weeks. Biweekly calls allow your customers to have time between each of your calls to work on their project or goal. The price that you can charge for coaching calls will depend largely on how big your audience is and what niche you're in. On the low end, you might charge $50 per hour for someone to talk directly to you. Some high-end consultants charge as much as $1,000 per hour to talk to them on the phone.

- **Freelancing and Productized Consulting** – If you have a valuable skill, such as web design, graphic design, audio editing, writing, editing, or programming, you can always sell your time for money. While I'm not a big fan of doing freelance work, many online entrepreneurs do freelance work when they are just getting started to generate some early revenue. A better way to do freelancing work is productized consulting, which sells a standardized service for a fixed fee. Productized consulting allows you to create teams and systems to handle orders, which allows you to eventually take yourself out of the equation. Kudu (www.kudu.io) is an example of a productized consulting service that manages your Google AdWords account for a fixed monthly fee.

- **Templates and Themes** – If you are a graphic designer or a web designer, you have the opportunity to sell WordPress themes, logos, patterns, brushes, and other web elements through websites like Theme Forest (www.themeforest.net). WordPress themes often sell for between $10 and $30, and logo templates often sell for between $5 and $20. The highest-grossing WordPress theme on Theme Forest has generated more than $200,000 in sales to date.

- **Subscriptions and Membership Websites** – Membership websites charge subscribers a fixed monthly fee to access a private community and content that is only available to members. Membership websites tend to charge between $5 and $100 per month, depending on the industry and what's included in the membership. A good example of a membership website is The Dynamite Circle (http://www.tropicalmba.com/dc), an online community of location-independent entrepreneurs that includes a discussion forum, mastermind groups, and a few in-person events each year.

- **Software-as-a-Service** – Software-as-a-Service, more commonly known as SaaS, is web-based software that users pay a recurring monthly fee to access. MailChimp, Dropbox, and Survey Monkey are examples of companies that use a software-as-a-service business model. Many online entrepreneurs love the idea of SaaS because of the recurring revenue. Most digital products earn money only once for each customer, but SaaS creates a reliable stream of income that comes whether or not you attract any new customers. SaaS can be incredibly lucrative, but it can also be a lot of work to develop a SaaS product that people want to pay for, and stay with. I would only consider creating a SaaS product after you have successfully created other types of digital products.

Why People Will Buy Digital Products from You

You might think that you won't be able to sell a digital product to your audience because there are people that know more than you, who are already selling better digital products than you could possibly put together yourself. You might also think that no one would buy any digital products from you because everything that you could teach is already on your website. You might even be afraid that you have nothing of value to offer. Many online entrepreneurs have these hang-ups, but they aren't valid reasons to give up on selling digital products before you even begin.

There are several reasons why your audience will buy products and services from you:

- **They want to learn something** – Some people see digital products as an alternative to participating in a class or a workshop that teaches them how to do something. Online courses, ebooks, and other digital products are attractive because they provide the opportunity to learn from an expert at one's own pace. Two different trends are fueling a boom in online learning—people value experiences much more than they used to, and companies are increasingly looking at what skills potential employees have over what degrees they have. By teaching people how to do things, you can help them create experiences for themselves, or help them become more attractive to potential employers.

- **They love you and can't get enough of you** – Oprah could recommend the worst book in the world and some people would still buy it, because they absolutely love Oprah, want to be like Oprah, and want to get their hands on everything that she makes and endorses. You probably won't build an audience the size of Oprah's, but if you create good content and inject your personality into it, a percentage of your audience will fall in love. They'll like your content so much that they will buy whatever digital products you create and sell, simply because they want to spend more time with you and your content. Even if there is a better digital product out there than the one you sell, they will buy your digital products because they want to learn from you.

- **They want convenicnce** – Even if all of your material is available for free on your website, some people will still buy an ebook or online course from you because they want all of the information in one place, that they can consume from start to finish. I would much rather pay $4.99 for an ebook or $100 for an online course that had all the best advice someone could give me than spend hours trying to dig through their website. Increasingly, people are recognizing how little time they have to work on hobbies and side projects, and are much more willing to pay for a package of information that helps them learn how to do something quickly and effectively.

- **They want to thank you** – Some people will have gotten so much value out of the content that you offer for free on your website, that they will buy something from you as a way of paying you for the value they have already gotten. They might not even intend to consume the digital product you sold them, but they want to give you some money as a way to say thank you for the value that you have created.

When to Start Selling Digital Products

Launching an online business requires an incredible amount of work over a long period of time, and there's never quite enough time to get everything done that you want to, so you have to be strategic about the projects that you tackle and when you want to tackle them. You should focus on the projects and tasks that will generate the most value for the least amount of work.

When you're first getting started with your online business, creating and trying to sell digital products is not a good use of your time. Trying to launch a digital product before you have an audience would be tantamount to trying to open a Wal-Mart on a deserted island. You might build the best product in the world, but it won't matter unless you have an audience that is ready and willing to buy something from you.

Calculating Critical Mass

Let's say that you want to create a $39 training guide that you can sell to your audience. For that price point, you might reasonably expect 0.5 percent to 2 percent of your email subscribers to purchase the product. If you have an email list of 1,000 subscribers, you can expect to generate between 5 and 20 sales.

On the other hand, if you have 25,000 subscribers and promote the same guide to your email list and receive similar conversion rates, you would sell between 125 and 500 copies of that same guide. At 1,000 subscribers, putting the effort into creating this guide probably isn't worth it because of the time required to write, edit, format, and market the guide. You are only going to make a few hundred dollars, and that is if your training guide sells well. At 25,000 subscribers, it's almost certainly worth it to create the guide, because you could make nearly $20,000 in sales if it converts well.

In most cases, I wouldn't recommend launching digital products until you have about 10,000 subscribers. If you're not there yet, just focus on creating great content and marketing that content so that you can continue to grow your audience until it reaches the right size. When you hit 10,000 subscribers, the revenue you can generate from creating and selling products will justify the amount of time it takes to create, launch, and market digital products. This isn't a hard and fast rule, but I wouldn't try to create a unique digital product and try to launch it to a list of much less than 10,000 people, simply because it wouldn't be worth the effort to do so.

In 2014, I purchased an equity stake of USGolfTV, a company that produces training content and digital products for the golf industry. The other owners were interested in launching a membership site, but at the time they had less than 5,000 subscribers. I knew they would likely only sell a handful of memberships at that list size, so I told them to focus on growing their list for a year and helped them implement strategies that would attract more opt-ins.

About a year later, they had grown their email list to more than 50,000 subscribers and successfully launched a one-off video course in the interim. By that point, it had become worth it to explore creating a membership site. We put about 6 months of work into creating content and launching a membership site called My Virtual Golf Coach (www.myvirtualgolfcoach.com), and immediately garnered a large number of sign-ups because we had a sizable email list and created a product that met our audience's needs.

How to Develop an Idea for Your Digital Product

The same strategies that you use to identify what kind of content to create on your website can be used to identify what kind of digital products to create. You can create products based on what your competitors are doing, build products around the issues that people in your niche are talking about on Quora and public discussion forums, or offer products that simply cover the basics.

However, the best way to determine what digital product you create is to—as I suggested in Chapter Four—ask your audience what they are struggling with and build a product that specifically addresses that issue.

For example, at USGolfTV we regularly hear from golfers who slice the ball when they swing (meaning the ball does not fly straight and hooks off to one side or another). To address this issue, we launched a product called Tour Draw that teaches golfers exercises and strategies that they can implement to get rid of their slice, have their drives fly straight down the fairway, and hit the ball further than they would otherwise. Because we built a product that specifically met the needs that our audience told us they had, it sold extremely well relative to some of the other digital products the company launched.

If you don't know what problems your audience is facing, send them an email survey and ask them what they need help with. Keep your survey short so that you actually get a good number of responses. You can either use Survey Monkey (www.surveymonkey.com) to collect responses, or simply have your audience email you directly. Make sure to ask open-ended questions, so that your readers have the opportunity to really share their mind. Finally, make sure to thank them for helping out by letting them know how much you appreciate them.

Here is an example of a survey email I sent to my list a while back:

Hi [Name] -

Since you're a subscriber to our daily newsletter, I wanted to give you a heads up about something new that we're going to offer later in the month.

We're putting together a 40 to 50 page guide that will tentatively be called The Trader's Guide to Equities Research, which will help you get a better understanding of how to make trading decisions with information in our daily reports. You'll also get a much a better understanding of which brokerages you should listen to and which you should ignore, with some new rankings data that we've never made available before.

We want to make sure that we put as much value in this guide as possible and want to make sure that it's something that will be helpful to you and other newsletter subscribers.

So, if you have a moment, I have a couple of questions I'm hoping you could help answer:

- *How do you decide which analyst ratings you should pay attention to?*
- *What questions do you have about investing, stock ratings or equities research?*
- *What information could we offer to you to that would help you trade more effectively?*

Simply respond to this email with your responses. I'll incorporate as much of the feedback as I can into the guide we're putting together.

Thanks!

Matthew Paulson
MarketBeat.com

When you begin to get feedback from your audience about what problems they face, focus on the issues that you hear about over and over again. You should probably disregard topics that you only hear about from one person, because you don't know if other people in your niche face that same problem. When you hear independently from multiple people about the same issue, you know it's a problem that's common for many members of your audience. For every one person that tells you about an issue they're having, there's probably ten more that didn't take the time to email you back and tell you they're having that same issue.

After you have gathered some ideas from your audience about what kind of digital product to create, make sure that your idea is big enough to constitute a standalone digital product. If you could cover the topic in its entirety in a 1,500-word blog post, the idea may not be broad enough to constitute a digital product. You want your audience to feel like they've really learned a lot after buying and consuming your digital product. Try to choose topics that you can really dive into in detail and write 10,000 to 20,000 words about. Having a larger topic will enable you to create an information-rich digital product that provides your audience a lot of value.

Creating Your Digital Product

Before you begin creating an outline and writing or recording videos, the first step to creating your digital product is writing the marketing copy you plan on using to promote it later on landing pages and in pitch emails. By writing your marketing copy first, then building a product using the marketing copy as a guide, you will avoid the risk of failing to deliver on what your marketing promises or building a product that can't be marketed effectively.

Your marketing copy should explain what your product teaches, who should buy it, why they should buy it, and what features and benefits come along with the product. This is a big picture statement about the product and its promises to the customer. In a way, your marketing copy will serve as a mini-outline that will help determine what should be included in your product. You can view the copy that we use for MarketBeat Daily Premium, MarketBeat's core digital product, at www.MarketBeat.com/subscribe/subscribe.aspx

After your marketing copy has been written, the next step is to create a full outline for your digital product. Your outline should contain all of the major topics that you want to cover, along with all of the points that you want to cover under each topic. Your outline should be about 10 percent of the length of the end product that you plan on creating. If you want to create a 10,000-word PDF guide, your outline should be about 1,000 words, broken out in bullet points. While creating a detailed outline can be a lot of work, you'll be able to completely avoid writer's block when you are actually creating your product, because you will know exactly what you are going to write about.

After your outline has been created, choose the type of digital product that's most appropriate for your website, whether that be an ebook, a video course, a membership site, a newsletter, productized consulting, or a SaaS offering. For topics that don't change very often, ebooks and video courses are a solid way to deliver content. For topics that change regularly or have new information coming out, you can either do a paid newsletter or a membership website, and charge a recurring monthly fee for access. For ideas that require hands-on work or need to be tailored to each individual customer, consider doing productized consulting or a SaaS offering.

Only choose a product type that you are comfortable creating. If you're not good on video, don't create a video course. If you have no idea how to create software or hire developers, don't create a SaaS product. Even if your content is great, poor presentation and execution will ruin your product's chances of success. If you aren't comfortable creating the type of digital product that's best suited for your topic, choose the next most appropriate product type that you are comfortable doing. Personally, I would have a hard time recording myself on video jabbering on about a topic—that's why I write books.

Once your outline is written, you have chosen what kind of product you are going to create, and you know how you plan on publishing your content—whether that be through Gumroad, your own website, or another solution—you can begin to actually create your content. Product creation is a lot of work and it may take several weeks for you to create a high-quality digital product.

In order to actually get your product finished, commit to creating content every day until the product is complete. You must create a habit out of content creation and force yourself to work on your product daily. When I'm working on a new book, I commit to writing 1,000 words every single day and do my writing first thing in the morning so that if I get nothing else done in a day, I will have made some progress in my book. By making writing my first priority every day, I'm guaranteed to make forward progress and actually get my book written in a reasonable amount of time.

Once your product is fully written, recorded, or otherwise put together, have a few friends or some of your superfans look it over and test it out. Have them check for grammatical issues, typos, and anything else that would cause your product to come across as unprofessional. Make sure that all of the links in your product and any embedded videos work properly. Go through the ordering and checkout process yourself to make sure that buying and consuming your product is a simple and straightforward process. Test out your product as much as you can to avoid having major hiccups when it comes time to formally launch your product.

How to Have a Successful Product Launch

In order to successfully launch a product to your audience, you need to make a really big deal about your launch and give your audience incentives to buy during your launch period.

The best way to make sure that your audience knows about your new product or service is by advertising it to your email list. You will also want to involve your other platforms, such as your website and social media profiles, but your email list will probably be the primary source for the vast majority of the sales. You'll want to send email messages to your audience about your product as it's being developed, when it's close to being ready, and when it's available to purchase.

As you begin working on the product, send an update once or twice a month about what's going on and how close it is to being launched. When you are about a month away from your launch, send emails that will start getting people excited. Tell them about the features and benefits of your product, how much the product will cost, when the launch will be, how the product will benefit them, what they get when they buy, etc. You should also include screenshots, a sample video, or an excerpt from your product so they can get a better feel for what it will be like.

Try to send out one pre-launch email a week for the four weeks leading up to your launch, with the last email being a few days before your product comes out. Each new email should contain some information that hasn't been previously revealed, like pricing, the launch date, or the bonuses they will get if they buy during the launch period.

When it comes time to launch your product, establish a specific time period with a defined end date during which users will receive a special incentive for buying. This is known as your launch period. Your launch period can be anywhere from two weeks to a month. For your special incentive, you can offer some kind of add-on bonus that will only be available during this time. For a bonus, you could offer a short ebook, training videos, or anything else that your audience may perceive as valuable.

Don't assume that you have to spend a lot of time on your bonus either. You might already have an older product you can use as your bonus, or you might be able to compile some information you have already created. For a previous book, I offered a collection of audio interviews that I had done previously. These interviews had already been recorded and produced, I just packaged them together into a single file that readers could listen to at their leisure.

The other way to incentivize your users is to offer a time-limited discount during your launch period. For example, you could give your audience a 20 percent discount if they purchase your product within the first 30 days of its availability.

If you are wary of cutting the price of your product, just raise the base price by 20 percent and then offer a 20 percent discount. You will receive the exact same pricing you had previously planned, but your customers will feel like they are getting a discount.

This is what major department stores do by listing high sticker prices and then discounting them heavily. You do have to be careful about offering too many discounts, because you might inadvertently be training your customers to only buy stuff from you when it's on sale.

During your launch period, send out a series of emails to your audience about your product. In *40 Rules for Internet Business Success*, I created a sample schedule for emails that people can use to base a product launch email series off of. While I wrote that series more than two and a half years ago, it works as well today as it did then. I still use it as the basis for my new product launches.

Instead of writing a new launch email series for this book, I've decided to include the same 49-day sample launch schedule I've used in the past:

- **28 Days Before Launch**: Announce your launch date and tell your audience about the features and benefits of your product.

- **21 Days Before Launch**: Answer a list of frequently asked questions about your product.

- **14 Days Before Launch**: Provide a video tour, screencast of your product, (if it's a video course), offer sample videos, or (if it's an ebook) an excerpt of your product.

- **7 Days Before Launch**: Announce the bonuses that users will receive if they register during the launch period.

- **1 Day Before Launch**: Reminder of launch date/time, bonuses and pricing.

- **Launch Day**: Announce that the product is available and provide a link to sign up for the product.

- **4 Days After Launch Day**: Send another email that contains the answers to the frequently asked questions about your product.

- **8 Days After Launch Day**: Send your subscribers some social proof (often in the form of testimonials) about the rave reviews your product has received.

- **12 Days After Launch Day**: Remind your users of what pain your problem solves and the features and benefits of your product.

- **16 Days After Launch Day**: Remind your users about the bonuses and discount they'll receive if they sign up during the launch period.

- **20 Days After Launch Day**: Announce that tomorrow is the last day to receive the discount and bonus.

- **21 Days After Launch Day**: Announce that the launch period is ending today and that it's the last day to get the discount and bonus.

It is important to have a defined end date to your launch period. Many of your readers will purchase your product right away, but some of your audience members will procrastinate and wait until the last possible moment to purchase your product. By having a clearly defined end date, you create a sense of urgency to encourage your readers to buy your product, before the discount and any bonuses that you offer are no longer available. If you have a clearly-defined end date to your launch and send emails to your audience warning them that the incentive is ending soon, as many as 25 percent of your launch customers will buy your product during the last couple days. What can I say? Some people are procrastinators.

In addition to using your email list, you will want to leverage any other channels that you have to communicate with your audience. This will include any social networks that you publish content to, as well as your website.

When your product launches, you should publish a new blog post that talks about the product, what it includes, why users should buy it, and provide a link to purchase the product. Also include a prominent ad for your product in the sidebar of your website that directs users over to your product's landing page where they can learn about your product. For your social media channels, you will probably want to publish something about your product launch every day, or every other day, during your launch period. Using your social media channels will help remind your readers to take action, and allow you to reach members of your audience that aren't on your email list.

You can also promote your product by doing a podcast tour. By getting yourself booked to be interviewed on other people's podcasts, you will have an opportunity to talk about your product to someone else's audience. If the podcast host is willing to overtly promote your product, you can give them an affiliate commission for any sales that they generate. Not all podcast hosts will be willing to do this, so you may need to send out several inquiries to find a host that will be willing to let you talk about your product.

When sending out interview inquiries, be mindful of each podcast's audience size because it may not be worth the effort to be interviewed by podcasters that have a small audience. A good way to verify that a podcast has an audience is to look at the number of iTunes reviews the podcast has. Make sure the podcast has at least 50 reviews, and a few that were submitted in the last few months.

How to Organize Your Product Launch

Between the website posts, email messages, social media status updates, podcast interviews, ad campaigns, and any other promotion that you plan on doing, it can be difficult to keep track of all of the things you will be doing to promote your product during its launch period. In order to stay organized, I use the paper calendar method discussed in Chapter Four to organize all my messaging for the month(s) of the product launch. I pencil in every email message, social media share, blog post, and all other marketing activities on the day that they need to happen.

When the launch period happens, I simply go through the activities for each day and make sure that I get them taken care of. If you want to get ahead of the game, you can write your emails and social media status updates ahead of time and pre-schedule them, using Buffer.com for your social media updates and your email service provider for your email messages.

Tools to Facilitate Your Product Launch and Sales

There are several companies that produce software and services geared toward people selling digital products.

Here are some software packages and services you might consider using as part of your product launch:

- **ClickBank** – ClickBank (www.clickbank.com) is an established platform for selling digital products, such as ebooks, tools and guides. ClickBank will process orders for your digital products and deliver them to customers after purchase. ClickBank has a built-in affiliate marketing network, where other website owners can promote your products to their audience in exchange for a commission for each sale that they generate. ClickBank charges a transaction fee of 7.5 percent of the sale price, plus $1.00 for each transaction.

- **ClickFunnels** – ClickFunnels (www.clickfunnels.com) is a web-based sales funnel creation platform, useful for collecting email opt-ins and selling products. ClickFunnels offers a friendly drag-and-drop interface and numerous templates that you can use to create landing pages and checkout pages quickly and painlessly. ClickFunnels is sold on a subscription basis and starts at $97 per month.

- **Creative Market and Envato Market** – Creative Market (www.creativemarket.com) and Envato Market (market.envato.com) are two digital marketplaces that allow designers, developers, and other creators to sell things like WordPress themes and plugins, logo templates, audio clips, original photography, fonts, 3D rendering assets, and more.

- **Gumroad** – Gumroad (www.gumroad.com) is a service that facilitates the sale and delivery of digital products. You can use Gumroad for your digital product's checkout and ordering process. Gumroad will process payments on your behalf, and automatically deliver your digital product to your customer after purchase. Gumroad also offers some unique features, like lightweight digital rights management tools that discourages sharing of your products, license key creation, support for multiple currencies, and a "pick your price" option. Gumroad charges creators $10 per month to use their platform, plus a transaction fee of 3.5 percent, plus 30 cents per charge.

- **Leadpages** – Leadpages (www.leadpages.com) is the industry standard landing page creation software. You can use Leadpages' drag-and-drop interface to easily create attractive landing pages that will push readers to sign up for your email list and buy your products. Leadpages is sold on a subscription basis and starts at $25 per month.

- **MemberMouse** – MemberMouse (www.membermouse.com) is a WordPress plugin that transforms your website into a membership website. The software creates a password-protected members-only portion of your website, facilitates the checkout and signup process for your membership site, and integrates with a variety of payment providers to handle recurring payments. MemberMouse also comes with solid reporting software that will help you track important metrics, such as lifetime customer value, retention rates, and refunds. MemberMouse is sold on a subscription basis and starts at $19.95 per month.

- **Stripe** – Stripe (www.stripe.com) is a credit card processing company that caters to software developers and online businesses. Stripe integrates with most shopping cart and membership website software packages. Stripe has an extensive API, which makes it very easy for developers to integrate into their existing software. Stripe can also process Bitcoin and ACH Payments. Stripe has no monthly fees, and charges a credit card transaction fee of 2.9 percent of the charge amount, plus 30 cents per transaction.

- **Udemy** – Udemy (www.udemy.com) is an online education platform that allows anyone to publish their own online courses. Udemy features state-of-the-art design tools that make creating an online course as simple as uploading your video recordings and your other content to their website. Udemy processes customer payments for you and handles all aspects of the delivery of your course and customer service. As a course creator, you keep 100 percent of the revenue when you promote your course and 50 percent of the revenue when Udemy promotes your course for you.

- **WooCommerce** – WooCommerce (www. woocommerce.com) is a WordPress add-on that integrates ecommerce functionality into your existing website. You can use WooCommerce to set up a shopping cart or sell digital products through your existing website. The primary benefit of using WooCommerce over another service to sell your digital products is that your customers can purchase products without ever having to leave your website. WooCommerce integrates with Stripe, Authorize.Net, and many other payment providers. WooCommerce is also very extensible and comes with its own ecosystem of plugins and themes. WooCommerce itself is free, but there are a variety of plugins and themes for WooCommerce that cost money.

How to Generate Sales Post Launch

You might generate a large number of sales during your initial launch period only to find that sales taper off after the promotional efforts for your launch conclude. You might be worried that you won't be able to generate meaningful sales from your digital products after launch, and think that you will have to create another new product to generate any additional sales. Fortunately, this is not the case.

There are a number of strategies that you can use to continue to generate sales for your existing digital products over time:

- **Use your autoresponder series** – Add a variation of some of the promotional emails you used during your product launch to your autoresponder series. Your digital product will be automatically marketed to your new subscribers when they hit the appropriate day in your series. New subscribers will not have been on your list during your digital product's initial launch, so the autoresponder emails they receive will likely be the first time that they hear about your product.

- **Create a products page on your website** – In your website's main navigation, there should be a page called products that highlights all of the digital products that you have produced and sold. For each product that you have created, you should include a description of the product, along with its logo or any other promotional graphics you used during launch, and a link to buy it. This will give people that are clicking around your website looking for more content an opportunity to find your paid products.

- **Offer time-limited discounts on your products** – We regularly discount our subscription products during the weekend after Thanksgiving as a way to boost sales during a week that might otherwise be slow for digital products. By only making the discount available for a few days, you can create a sense of urgency for potential customers that are on the fence. If they want to buy your product at the discounted price, they will have to take action and make their purchase before your sale is over.

- **Relaunch one of your existing products** – Simply go through the content of one of your existing products, make any updates that are necessary, and add an additional section or two of content to the product. When you re-launch an existing product, you can send a two-week or three-week email campaign, just like you would when you are launching a new product.

Make sure to give everyone that purchased the first iteration of your product a free copy of the new version, because your audience will revolt if you expect them to pay full price for a slightly updated product. You should only re-launch a product about a year after your last launch. This will allow for plenty of time for new people to subscribe to your mailing list that weren't subscribed during your initial launch.

- **Launch new products** – If your existing products are no longer selling that well, you can always create a new product. While starting over from scratch on a brand new digital product may be a lot of work, it will serve as another long-term digital asset that you can use to generate revenue for your business.

Action Steps

- Determine what metrics you will use to determine if your business is large enough to successfully launch a digital product.

- Brainstorm ideas for potential digital products your company can sell.

- Survey your audience and ask them what they most need help with in your niche.

- When your business is big enough, conceptualize, outline, and create your first digital product.

- Sign up for Gumroad or another service that will process orders for your digital products.

- Write your launch email series and launch your first digital product.

CHAPTER EIGHT

*Creating Systems and
Building a Great Team*

YOU MAY BE ABLE to grow your business to $100,000 to $250,000 in annual revenue by working hard, learning a lot, and implementing the strategies outlined in the first seven chapters of this book. However, in order to get past the $250,000 mark in annual revenue, you need an entirely different set of skills.

Your personal hustle will only take your online business so far, because you only have so many hours to work in a week, and you can't become an expert at running every aspect of your online business. When you run out of hours in a week and don't have any systems or people to help you, your business will stop growing. As your business grows, you need to establish systems and build a team that can run the day-to-day operations, so that different aspects of your business can thrive without your direct involvement.

In this chapter, you will learn:

- Why working in your business will slow down your company's growth.

- How to find and hire your first team members.

- Strategies to effectively manage and lead your team.

- How to use standard operating procedures to get consistent quality work.

Working on Your Business vs. Working in Your Business

There are two broad categories of work related to your business—working on your business and working in your business. If you have read the book *E-Myth* by Michael Gerber, you already know what I'm talking about.

Working *on* your business includes any type of work that will push forward its long-term future success. These tasks include hiring employees, leading your team, finding new revenue sources, establishing systems, negotiating business development deals, and long-term strategic planning. Completing tasks that fall under working on your business won't move the needle on any of the day-to-day tasks, but they will position your company for long-term growth and success.

Working *in* your business involves doing the day-to-day tasks of running your business. In the online business world, these tasks include creating content, managing your website, doing graphic design work, managing your company's books, moderating comments on your website, and any other tasks that aren't directly related to growing your audience, generating revenue, leading your people, or establishing systems.

If you are a one-woman or one-man show, it can be very easy to get bogged down completing the day-to-day tasks of running your business. You might be so focused on the current customer or the next blog post that you never get around to doing any planning that will establish your business for long-term success.

You can do all of the day-to-day work in the world, but your business won't continue to grow without long-term strategic planning, building a team and establishing systems. Conversely, if you do all the planning in the world, but never actually do the hands-on tasks of getting your business off the ground, you will fail before you even launch.

Early on in your business, the key is to recognize when you are working *in* your business versus when you are working *on* your business, and making time for both categories of tasks. Over time, you will begin to build a team to handle the day-to-day operations so that you can spend more time working on the long-term growth of your business.

You Need a Team

Your online business will require a unique combination of skills, including vision casting, writing, editing, graphic design, social media marketing, website management, ad selection and placement, product creation, and customer service. Nobody is good at doing everything and chances are, there are some skills in that list that you are pretty bad at or simply don't want to do. If you want your business to grow and get better over time, bring on people that are smarter than you to handle the parts of your business that you are bad at.

I'm not very good at web design and front-end development, so I employ a full-time web designer. I'm also not terribly excited about answering the 25 to 50 customer support emails that come into MarketBeat every day, so I've hired a dedicated customer support person that can handle those emails with excellence. By hiring out those two positions, my business has a much better website and is much better at customer service than if I were trying to do everything myself. By delegating these two roles, I also have more time to focus on the things that I'm best at and the things that drive revenue for MarketBeat.

You also must recognize that your time is more valuable than you think it is. If you made $100,000 this year, the effective value of your time would be $50 an hour (assuming you work 40 hours per week for 50 weeks out of the year). If your time is worth $50 per hour, you probably shouldn't be doing work that you can easily hire out for $15 an hour. This is why I never mow my own lawn or try to do any household repairs myself—I'd much rather write a small check and have someone else worry about mowing my lawn or fixing my shower.

You might be able to replace the work that you are hiring out at a relatively-low hourly rate with more valuable tasks that generate more revenue for your business. But be careful, because this is a situation where you almost always get what you pay for. Even if that's not the case, you still might want to pay $15 to $25 an hour to someone else to free up an hour of time to do things that you enjoy.

Your First Hire

You might think that you don't have enough work to keep an employee or contractor busy or that you can't afford to bring on a team member right now. Many entrepreneurs that have never hired before have these two hang-ups and it stops them from ever building a team. You are right, you probably can't afford to hire anyone and keep them busy when you are first getting started, but this will change over time as your business grows.

Eventually, you will be able to keep a team member busy and even have plenty of revenue to pay their salary. The key is to know when you've hit that point and should make your first hire.

The rule of thumb that I use is that you should hire someone when you have three months of their salary in the bank and you can fill up at least half of their work load. If you are considering bringing on a full-time employee that will cost $4,000 per month in salary, benefits, and payroll taxes, try to have at least $12,000 in your bank account so that you know for sure you can take care of their first several paychecks. This financial buffer will give your new employee some time to create financial impact in your business so that their work covers their salary and then some. If you have made a good hire, your employees will pay for themselves several times over and you won't have to worry about how to pay them. The combination of your freed-up time and the value they create in your business will be able to cover their salary after a few months.

If you are worried about whether or not you can keep a new team member busy, make the hire when you can fill up at least 50 percent of their time. If you have 20 hours per week for a new full-time employee to do, you can safely make the hire because their responsibilities and workload will grow over time as your business grows. Small employers also often tend to underestimate how much time specific tasks take because they have been doing said tasks themselves for years and have the process down cold. A relatively new employee will take longer to do the same task that you have been doing because they haven't been doing it for years.

If you're not sure how many hours you can give an employee, give them a range of hours per week of work you think you'll have for them. When I hired my first part-time employee, I had no idea how long it would take her to do the work I was delegating to her. I thought it would take 20 hours per week for her to do the job, so I told her I could give her 15-25 hours per week of work, and told her that number would probably grow over time as the business grows. You can also start an employee off as part-time and tell them the opportunity can grow into a full time job over the course of several months.

When to Hire Contractors vs. Employees

In the United States, there are two broad categories of workers—employees and independent contractors. Employees tend to work for a single company and contractors tend to do a very specific task, such as graphic design or accounting, for multiple businesses. Employees work hours set by their employer and contractors are free to set their own hours. Employees can receive employment benefits and contractors do not. Employees generally work at their employer's place of business and independent contractors are free to work wherever they want. The IRS has established specific guidelines that determine when a worker can be classified as an employee or an independent contractor. You can read more about these rules on the IRS website or by searching "employees vs. contractors" in your search engine of choice.

In my business, I currently have two employees other than myself, and a number of contractors that work on specific projects for me. Generally, you would hire an independent contractor when you have a small project that has a defined end date. For example, if you want to have your website redesigned, you are probably going to hire someone as a contractor and not an employee, because after your website is complete, you won't have any more work for them. People that perform the same task for many other companies—such as legal services or accounting—will probably be hired as independent contractors, too.

For people that are going to work a large number of hours in your business that you have to train, it just makes sense to hire them on as employees and run payroll. Some entrepreneurs try to save a bit of money by classifying people as contractors that really should be labeled as employees, but this is not a good idea. When you do this, you are only saving money because you are shifting some of your tax burden onto your team member. The IRS may also come after you for labeling people as contractors that really should be employees.

If you have never hired an employee before and run payroll, it can be a scary process at first. You may have to submit your new hire to your state. They will need to give you a W-4 form and you will need to take money out of their paycheck and send it to the IRS. You will need to pay state and federal unemployment tax, too.

There is a bit of a learning curve to running payroll, but you don't actually have to know how to do any of this stuff yourself. You can hire ADP (www.adp.com), PayChex (www.paychex.com), or a local accountant to run payroll on your behalf. You can tell them what hours your employee worked and they'll take care of all the forms and filing for you, for a small fee. There are even companies that will help set up and manage a 401(k) plan and health insurance for your employees.

Please do not rely on this chapter as your only resource when it comes to hiring and working with contractors because I don't know anything about your specific situation and I have no specific professional training on employment law. If you have questions about whether or not someone should be considered a contractor or employee, or have a question about how to hire an employee, take the time to check with your state department of labor or another qualified professional to get specific advice about your business.

What to Delegate and Outsource

If you are at your maximum workload capacity and are looking to bring someone on to lighten your load, make a list of your current work-related responsibilities and how much time each of those responsibilities takes each week. You can use a tool like RescueTime.com to track your computer usage, and tell you what applications and websites you spend the most time using each week to automate this process.

After you have your list of responsibilities, highlight the ones that you don't like doing, the ones that you are not particularly good at, and the ones that aren't a good use of your time. The responsibilities that get highlighted are the tasks that you should try to outsource or hire a team member to do first.

For example, let's say that you hate doing your company's bookkeeping, processing invoices, and paying your company's bills. Like myself and most entrepreneurs, you're probably not very good at these tasks. These three responsibilities would be very low-hanging fruit to outsource or delegate, because they are not one of your core competencies, and you can easily hire someone to do them for you. You could group these three tasks together into a single part-time position, or you could hire an outside accounting firm to do these tasks for you on a contract basis. Hiring a bookkeeper/accountant was one of the best early hires my company made. By having someone else who knows what they are doing keep the IRS and my state's taxing authorities at bay, I don't have to worry about filing dates and whether or not I'm going to screw up a government form. Thus, I can actually focus on running my business.

Of course, there are a lot of different things that you can hire an employee to do, or have someone do for you on a contract basis. In the online business world, you can hire a personal assistant to manage your email, schedule appointments for you, book travel, and complete other basic administrative tasks.

You can hire a customer service person to handle the incoming customer support requests that your business receives. You can hire a designer to do graphic and web design work. If you want to add custom functionality to your website or create a mobile app, you can hire a developer. You can bring on additional writers to supplement the content that you create.

However, there are some things that you should never try to outsource or delegate.

What You Can't Delegate or Outsource

Never try to outsource or delegate anything that is a core competency of your business, or is one of your business's competitive advantages. Core competencies are fundamental components of your business that you need to know better than anyone else in order for your business to be successful, such as marketing and product development.

For example, if you were to create a business selling the finest hand-made watches in the world, you wouldn't be able to outsource watch manufacturing because it is the primary core competency of the business. If you are going to be a watch manufacturer and are going to have another company do the actual watch manufacturing for you, your business doesn't need to exist . For your business to succeed, you simply cannot outsource the central components if you present yourself as knowing how to do them better than everyone else.

Here are some things that you should not outsource in your online business:

- **Vision, Mission and Culture** – As the owner of a business, you must design the vision, mission and culture for your company. You are the captain, and no one else can steer your ship and set a course for your company but you. What your business stands for has to come from the top, and it has to be communicated to your team and your audience over and over again so that it sticks. You can't hire someone and make them responsible for the culture and overall direction of your business, unless you plan on firing yourself and making them the CEO of the company.

- **Marketing** – Don't hire a general marketing agency to do the marketing for your online business. They may be more than willing to take your money, but they probably won't take responsibility for the results of their work. Just try asking a marketing agency to work for you on a performance basis—all of them will say no. You need to take primary responsibility for the marketing of your business, learn the strategy involved, be able to test different marketing channels, and measure your results. You can hire a designer to assemble ads and other marketing creative for you, but you need to take primary responsibility for the success or failure of your marketing efforts. No one knows your business better than you.

- **Product Creation** – You have to own the vision of your digital products and take primary responsibility for putting them together. You need to be the person that outlines your digital product, creates the majority of the content, and markets your digital product to your audience. You can certainly get help with the design, layout and technical aspects, but you need to own the message and marketing of your digital products. If you outsource the core of your digital products, it won't have the same passion, enthusiasm, and insight as it would if you were to create it yourself. It also wouldn't be your digital product, because you weren't the one that created it!

- **Early Content Creation** – You have to write at least the first 100 articles on your website yourself.

By creating all of the content early on, you are establishing a voice and vision for your brand. Until the vision, mission, and values of your brand are firmly established, you shouldn't bring on anyone else to create content for your business because they won't know what your business is all about, how you write, what kind of content your readers expect, and what level of quality work they are expected to produce.

Referrals Lead to Great Team Members

I have probably hired about two dozen people between employees and contractors over the course of the last decade. I have never created a single job posting or used a website like Freelancer.com or Upwork.com to find a contractor.

Job posting websites certainly have their place, but I have always been able to find solid contractors and employees through personal networking and getting recommendations from friends and business acquaintances. I have been able to build a pretty wide network of business contacts over the last decade as a result of going to conferences, participating in online discussion groups, and taking a lot of coffee meetings. Whenever I need to hire someone new, I first try to think if there's anyone that I already know that I can hire. If no one comes to mind, I ask friends that also run online businesses if they know anyone that might be good for the position. If I couldn't get a good referral, I might then turn to a job posting website or public Facebook groups that I am a part of.

But so far I haven't had to go that route. In almost every case, I have known someone, or gotten a solid recommendation from a business acquaintance, and been able to fill the position.

If you don't have a wide network of business acquaintances that you can ask for recommendations from, you can shortcut this process by joining a few select Facebook groups geared toward online business owners. Specific Facebook groups serve as a discussion board for online business owners, and people regularly share recommendations for contractors and employees. After joining these groups, write a new post, share what kind of position you need to fill, and see if anyone has a recommendation for someone that you can hire.

While you can get a lot of good help in these groups, remember these groups don't solely exist to help you. Make sure that you are giving value to others as well, and not just collecting tips on how to improve your own business.

Here are some Facebook groups you might join if you need recommendations for contractors or employees:

- **Rhodium Community for Online Entrepreneurs**
https://www.facebook.com/groups/rhodiumcommunity

- **The Smart Passive Income Community**
https://www.facebook.com/groups/spicommunity

- **Zero to Scale: The Journey to $100,000 Per Month and Beyond**
https://www.facebook.com/groups/zerotoscale

- **Internet Marketing Super Friends**
https://www.facebook.com/groups/imsuperfriends

- **The Startup Chat**
https://www.facebook.com/groups/TheStartupChat

Making the Hire

If you have someone in mind for a contract or employment position, first ask them if they are interested in the work. If they are, give them a couple of test projects on a contract basis to see if they can follow your instructions, work independently, and produce quality work. Pay them for the test projects you have them do as you would any other contractor.

If they do a good job on your test projects, try to get some external feedback about the candidate from references they list and other people they have done work for that they haven't explicitly listed. Some of the best feedback you will get about someone will come from someone that they haven't listed as a reference. If your reference check comes back fine, their test project went well and you still want to hire them, you can then give them an offer letter.

An offer letter is a written document that outlines all pertinent information about a job, such as compensation, benefits, hours, responsibilities, location of work, whether or not the job requires travel, and any other expectations that you have for them as an employee. Your offer letter should also describe how their performance will be evaluated and under what circumstances they will get a raise.

In my offer letters, I state that they will be working for the company on a 90-day trial basis. After their 90-day trial period, they will either be offered a permanent position with the company or they will be let go. There's no legal requirement to include a statement like this in my state, but it sends a clear message to new employees that they will have to earn their keep if they want to stick around. Finally, your offer letter should include a deadline and instructions for them to accept the offer, which usually involves signing and returning the offer letter, completing a W-4 form, and attending an in-person training.

Managing Your Team

Many people think that managing others isn't hard and that they would be a pretty good boss given the opportunity, but creating an environment with good communication and healthy relationships where everyone does their best work won't happen by accident. Your goal should always be to be the person that everyone wants to work for, because happy team members will work hard for you and they won't jump ship.

Wouldn't it be great if your employees bragged to others about how great their job is? Wouldn't it be flattering if people came to you and asked if you have any positions open, because you have a reputation for being a great boss? These things are entirely possible, but you have to work at it.

Here are the techniques I use to lead my team members:

- **Set Clear Expectations** – There must a be a clear understanding between you and your team members about what you expect of them in terms of their quality of work, the volume of work they complete, and how they behave while they are at work or are otherwise representing your company. If both you and your employees are on the same page about these things, misunderstanding and miscommunication will be rare within your company.

- **Communicate Regularly** – Although my team members are remote, I touch base with them once per day to see what they are working on and how things are going. I try to encourage my team members to ask questions and tell me when they get stuck on something, so that I can step in and help when necessary. I also provide regular feedback about their quality of work so that they know whether they are doing well or need to step up their game. Our team uses a group messaging app called Slack (www.slack.com) to communicate back and forth throughout the day.

- **Recognize that Their Failure Is Your Fault** – If one of your team members does something wrong, it's more likely that it's your fault than theirs. If a team member screws up a task, it's probably because you didn't communicate your expectations well or you assigned the task to the wrong person. When a team member makes a mistake, don't scold them. Instead, ask them and yourself what you both could do differently to avoid making the same mistake in the future.

- **Surprise and Delight Your Team Members** – Every now and then, I will do something nice for my employees. I call these "actions of appreciation," and I do them simply because I genuinely appreciate them and want them to know that. Some examples of actions of appreciation include giving them an Amazon gift card, buying them movie tickets, having fresh flowers delivered to them, or giving them an unexpected bonus. Actions of appreciation don't even have to cost a lot of money. Spending $25 on movie tickets for your employee and their spouse a few times per year will be well worth the investment, because your employees will know that you value them and work harder for you as a result.

- **Don't Get Defensive When You Receive Negative Feedback** – If a team member (or anyone else for that matter) says something about you or your company that you don't agree with, don't retort and tell them why they're wrong. Your team members' perception of you is their reality. Take anything that you hear as feedback for improvement, rather than as a personal attack that needs to be responded to.

- **Give People Challenges Just Above their Current Skill Level** – Your team members should get better at what they do over time. The best way to do this is to give them challenges that are just beyond what they are currently capable of doing. Stretching them a little bit on each project will encourage them to learn new skills and will help them feel like they aren't in a rut doing the same type of work over and over again.

- **Help Make Your Employee's Dreams Come True** – One of the best pieces of advice I've gotten relating to managing employees is to ask your employees what their dreams are, then help to make them come true. If you can help your employees achieve their dreams, they will be fiercely loyal to you. For example, one of my employees told me that she wanted to do more than just design work, and wanted to learn to become a programmer. I paid $3,000 for her go to through a local code boot camp so she could get a good start on learning web programming. As a result of this investment, I have a higher-skilled, more valuable, and more loyal employee working for me.

- **Prioritize Your Projects** – At any given time, I might have two or three months' worth of work in queue for my employees to do. I do let them know everything that is currently on their plate so they can think about their upcoming projects in the back of their mind, but I always make sure that they know which projects are the highest priority. This way, they can focus on the tasks that will drive our business forward, in this moment. You can use something as simple as Google Doc or a shared Evernote document to list the projects and priorities for each employee's current queue of work.

Some of these techniques are unorthodox and aren't widely practiced in the business world, but they have worked very well for my business. By setting high expectations for my employees, compensating them well, and showing them how much I appreciate them, I have been able to get consistently good work from each of them.

Standard Operating Procedures

A standard operating procedures (SOP) is a written document that explains how people working at your company should complete a specific task, and why they should complete it in the way that you specify.

Your SOPs will also explain why you do things a certain way, which will allow your employees to better understand how you think and how you want your business run. SOPs effectively allow you to scale and work yourself out of the day-to-day operations, because you can ensure that this is exactly how you would complete the tasks yourself.. If your business uses SOPs and you have employee turnover or any other hire, you can use your SOP documents as training material, to help get the new employee up to speed more quickly.

SOP documents do not have to be complicated. Most of our SOPs are simple text documents that are less than 500 words in length, organized in a shared folder in Dropbox. Each SOP contains background information about why the task is important to the company, and why we complete that task in the manner that we do. Our SOPs also contain a set of steps to follow when completing that task, so that our team members can complete the task in a uniform and consistent manner. We try to create SOPs for tasks that are repeated at least once every other month so that we complete tasks consistently and correctly.

Here is an example of a standard operating procedure that we have in place for processing refunds:

Standard Operating Procedure for Responding to Refund Requests from MarketBeat Customers

Background: MarketBeat offers a variety of premium subscriptions that renew on either a monthly or annual basis, such as our daily newsletter (MarketBeat Daily Premium) and our research software (RatingsDB). All of our products come with a 30-day money-back guarantee, which offer our users a risk-free way to try out our software to see whether or not it's a good fit for them. Every now and then, someone will request a refund and you will have to decide whether or not to grant them the refund or not.

Refund Window: Our official refund window is 30 days, but you have flexibility to grant refunds up to 90 days if you determine that the situation warrants a refund (i.e. the user had problems accessing their subscription, their subscription was renewed and they didn't want it to renew, they're going to be a big pain to deal with, etc.). However, we do have to place some end date on offering refunds, because PayPal does not permit payments to be refunded after 60 days and our credit card provider does not permit refunds after 90 days.

Principles in Play:

- We stand by our word. Everyone that requests a refund within the first 30 days of their subscription—regardless of reason or circumstances—gets a refund.
- We don't need haters. We would rather give someone a refund than leave them with a negative image of our brand.

- You have permission to solve problems. You can solve any customer's problem without asking me, as long as it costs the company less than $200.00. If it's going to cost the company more than $200.00 to fix a customer's problem, check with Matt first.

Specific Instructions:

1. When a refund request comes in, check their subscription date to determine if they are eligible for a refund. If they would normally be eligible for a refund or if you believe there is good reason for them to receive a refund past the normal refund, move to step two. If they are not eligible for a refund and there is no compelling reason to stretch out our normal refund window, respond to their request using the "Refund Request – Denied" email template.

2. If a refund is approved, navigate to their account management page in our software system and find the payment in question. Click the "refund" button to process a refund back to their credit card. If the payment is more than 60 days old, you will need to manually refund the payment by logging into our PayPal account or our merchant account.

3. After you have processed the refund, send the customer using the "Refund Request – Approved" templates which lets them know that their refund has been processed and will appear in their account in the next five business days.

By having this standard operating procedure document for processing refunds, I know that my customer service team will consistently apply our refund policy, use the same principles that I would to determine whether or not to approve a refund, and use consistent messaging with each customer. If a new team member comes on board and they need to process a refund for the first time, they can refer to this SOP and follow the steps provided, without having to complete this task.

I truly believe that SOPs are a requirement for any business that is going to grow beyond six figures in annual revenue. You only have so many hours per day to work on your business and manage your employees. Having solid SOPs in place will ensure that your principles and processes for any given tasks are followed consistently for months and years down the line.

To learn more about standard operating procedures, I recommend reading the book *Work the System* by Sam Carpenter. The book teaches how to use a systems mindset in your business and create a series of systems and standard operating procedures so that your business can grow, scale, and succeed.

Wrap-Up

As your business grows and acquires more customers, there will be more work to do. Eventually, the amount of work required to run your business will outpace the time you have to work. At that point, you can either stop growing because you don't have time to do any more work than you are already doing, or you can begin to build a team.

You might be able to build a five-figure or six-figure online business without a team in place, but if you want to build a business that generates seven or eight figures in annual revenue, you must build a team of people that are smarter than yourself, and inspire them to work together toward a unified vision. At the same time, you must begin to establish systems and standard operating procedures so that your team completes work consistently and according to your business's vision, mission, and values.

For the first six years that I ran my business, I had no employees and only a couple of contractors working for me on a part-time basis. My business topped out at around $300,000 per year in revenue, but I couldn't seem to grow past that. It was only when I hired my first employee and began to bring on additional contractors that my business started to grow again.

It was three years ago that I hired my first employee. We've since hired an additional employee, and brought on several more contractors. Because we built the team and put systems in place, our revenue grew by a total of 900 percent during the following three years—earning us a spot on Inc. Magazine's list of the 5,000 fastest growing privately-held companies in the United States.

Action Steps

- Determine what criteria you will use to know when it's time to make your first hire.

- Make a list of tasks and responsibilities in your business that you would like to delegate or outsource.

- Never try to outsource marketing, product creation or your business's vision, mission and values.

- When your business hits the growth criteria that you set, bring on your first team member.

- Write your first standard operating procedure document.

CHAPTER NINE

Putting It All Together

THE POSSIBILITIES AHEAD OF you when you own a profitable online business are amazing. Eventually, you will have the freedom and flexibility to work where and when you want. If you want to take the afternoon off and play with your kids, do work around the house, or something else you enjoy, there's no one around to tell you that you can't do it. The extra income from your online business will allow you to pay off debt, save for retirement, and establish a college fund for your children or your grandchildren. You will be able to take a vacation without having to worry about whether or not you can afford it or have enough paid vacation days left in the year.

You will no longer have to answer to the whims of an employer and you will have the freedom to live your life how you choose.

There are a lot of great benefits to being a full-time entre-preneur who has a profitable online business, but you have to do the work to get there. In this final section, you will receive a step-by-step plan that you can follow to take action and launch your online business.

Fourteen Days to Launch Your Internet Business

This short chapter contains a 14-day launch plan that will help you get your business off the ground, with specific steps that you should take each day. At the end of your 14-day launch plan, you will have selected your niche, chosen a brand name, acquired a domain name, have built a fully functional website, written your first five articles, and have the beginnings of a prof-itable online business. Now, get to it and complete the tasks list-ed for day one.

Day One

- Develop a list of 20 to 30 different potential niches that could be the basis for your online business. Use the strategies outlined in the section "How to Identify Possible Niches" of Chapter One to come up with ideas.

- Later in the day, narrow your list of potential niche ideas down to the ten that you are most excited about pursuing. Focus on niches that align with your personal passion, but also have the potential to generate long-term profits.

Day Two

- Evaluate your 10 niche ideas using the decision matrix provided in Chapter One down to your top two or three.

- Sign up for a WordPress web hosting account with

DreamHost, BlueHost, GoDaddy, HostGator, or another web hosting provider.

Day Three

- It's decision time. Choose a single niche idea that you want to pursue for your online business, and move forward with only that idea.

- Brainstorm ideas for the name of your business using the strategies outlined in Chapter Two.

- Verify that each of your name ideas are not currently being used and are not already registered as trademarks by someone else.

Day Four

- Make a final decision about what name you want to use for your business. If you don't have a perfect name, don't worry. You can always transition to a better name down the road.

- Choose which social media networks and publishing channels you want to use for your online business.

- Identify and register the domain name that you want to use for your business using GoDaddy, Hover.com, or another domain name registrar.

Day Five

- Set up your domain on your hosting account, and use your web host's built-in tools to install WordPress onto your web hosting account. If you need help with this, don't hesitate to ask your web hosting provider to install WordPress for you.

- Sign up for accounts with the social networks that you want to use to promote your brand.

- Sign up for an account with Buffer.com so that you can pre-schedule your social media content.

Day Six

- Choose a WordPress theme for your website and upload it to your copy of WordPress.

- Install the list of must-have plugins listed in Chapter Three to your copy of WordPress.

- Write your website's about page. Your about page should be personal, include a picture of yourself, and communicate the vision and mission of your online business.

Day Seven

- Hire a local freelancer or use a service like 99 Designs or DesignContest.com to have a logo made for your business.

- Make a list of 20-30 topics that you can create content about on your website.

- Choose the top-level categories you want to use on your website, and set up your website's navigation menu.

Day Eight

- Write your first article and publish it on your website.

- Sign up for an account with an email service provider like MailChimp, Drip or Aweber.

- Set up your contact page. Include your email address, social media links, and a contact form.

Day Nine

- Write your second article and publish it on your website.

- Sign up for a publisher account with Google AdSense and one other ad network of your choosing.

Day Ten

- Write your third article and publish it on your website.
- Create the lead magnet that you will offer to readers in exchange for signing up for your mailing list.

Day Eleven

- Write your fourth article and publish it on your website.
- Add opt-in forms to your website using a plugin that integrates with your email service provider. Make sure that your opt-in forms reference the lead magnet that users will receive for signing up for your mailing list.

Day Twelve

- Write your fifth article and publish it on your website.
- Pre-schedule your first four posts along with other social media postings using Buffer.com.

Day Thirteen

- After your Google AdSense account has been approved, place three AdSense ads on your website using the best practices outlined in Chapter Six.
- Fill out the sidebar of your website with recent posts, social media links, archives and other relevant content.

Day Fourteen

- Develop a content schedule for your business using the process outlined in Chapter Four so that you continue to regularly post content on your website after your launch.

- Officially launch your website and start telling the world about your website.

You will note that there are only two or three items to complete each day. While it might seem like you can breeze through these tasks, many of them are very involved, and will take several hours. It's not easy to come up with a bunch of ideas for niches, your brand, and your domain name, and narrow them down to a single choice. Expect to put in at least three or four hours per day of work if you plan to complete this launch plan in the allotted fourteen days.

If you don't have that amount of time available, it's okay to complete the launch plan at a pace that better fits your schedule. Just recognize that it will take longer for your business to get off the ground if you don't put as many hours into growing your online business.

It's your move.

You have completed reading *Online Business from Scratch* and now it's time to take action. This book could be the next in a line of interesting books that you read but didn't do anything about, or it can be a catalyst for significant positive change in your life.

Think about where you want to be five years from now. The time will pass whether or not you build an online business.

Do you want to look back and be thankful that you took action, did the hard work, and built a profitable online business? Or do you want to be working the same job that you are today with the same dream of someday, just maybe, striking out on your own?

Online Business from Scratch has all of the information that you need to start and grow your authority publishing business; it's your time to take action.

THANK YOU

THANK YOU FOR READING *Online Business from Scratch* and choosing to spend some of your valuable time digging through the information I have to offer. I hope that this book will inspire you to take action and launch your own online business.

If you would like to share your thanks for this book, the best thing you can do is tell a friend about *Online Business from Scratch* or buy them a copy.

You can also show your appreciation for this book by leaving a review of the book on Amazon. To leave a review, visit the Amazon product page at www.FromScratchBook.com. Please be honest with your review, and with how this book has or has not helped you to achieve your goal of launching your own internet business. I want everyone to know if and how this book has changed your life in any significant way.

You can follow me online at my personal blog, MattPaulson.com. You can follow me on Twitter (@MatthewDP). You can follow me on Facebook at www.facebook.com/matthewpaulsonpage. I am also on LinkedIn (linkedin.com/in/matthewpaulson) and AngelList (angel.co/matthewpaulson).

If you would like to hear me talk about various topics, feel free to check out the interviews I have done at mattpaulson.com/interviews.

Thank you and God bless,

Matthew Paulson

November 1, 2016

ACKNOWLEDGMENTS

I **WOULD LIKE TO** express my sincere gratitude to my many friends, family members and business acquaintances who have encouraged me as I have pursued various entrepreneurial adventures over the last decade.

I would like to thank my wife, Karine, for being incredibly supportive, putting up with my unusual work schedule, and trusting me to provide for our family through my business.

I would like to thank my children, Micah and Adylin, for the joy that they bring into my life.

I would like to thank my business partners and team members, including David Anicetti, Donna Helling, Todd Kolb, Don Miller, Tyler Prins, Rebecca McKeever, Jason Shea, Stevie Shea and Toi Williams. Without them, my companies would not be where they are today.

Finally, I would like to express my gratitude to the many talented people who worked on this book.

I would like to thank Elisa Doucette and her team at Craft Your Content for editing this book and fixing my many grammar and spelling errors.

I would like to thank Rebecca McKeever for designing the cover of this book.

I would like to thank James Woosley for doing this book's layout.

I would like to thank Stu Gray for narrating the audio version of this book.

ABOUT THE AUTHOR

MATTHEW PAULSON IS THE founder of MarketBeat, a financial media company committed to making real-time investing information available to investors at all levels. MarketBeat publishes a daily investment newsletter to more than 400,000 subscribers and its network of financial news websites attracts more than 5 million visitors each month. MarketBeat's reporting has been covered by a number of major financial media outlets, including *Barron's Magazine*, the *Wall Street Journal*, *CNBC*, *MarketWatch* and *Seeking Alpha*.

Through his books, his personal blog, and his media appearances, Matthew teaches others about how to leverage the power of entrepreneurship in their lives and achieve personal financial freedom. Matthew's first two books, *40 Rules for Internet Business Success* and *Email Marketing Demystified*, teach readers some of the crucial steps to build profitable online businesses. Matthew's third book, *The Ten-Year Turnaround*, reveals how anyone can achieve financial freedom in ten years or less.

As an angel investor, Matthew has invested in a number of early-stage companies in a variety of verticals. He is also the chairman of Falls Angel Fund, a regional angel fund sponsored by the South Dakota Enterprise Institute, which has raised $1.2 million to invest in early-stage, high-growth companies in South Dakota and surrounding states.

Matthew holds a B.S. in Computer Science and an M.S. in Information Systems from Dakota State University. He also holds an M.A. in Christian Leadership from Sioux Falls Seminary.

Matthew resides in Sioux Falls, South Dakota, where he lives with his wife, Karine, and his two children, Micah and Adylin.

Connect with Matthew at:

- Matthew's Personal Blog: www.MattPaulson.com
- AngelList: www.angel.co/matthewpaulson
- Facebook: www.facebook.com/matthewpaulsonpage
- LinkedIn: www.LinkedIn.com/in/matthewpaulson
- Twitter: www.twitter.com/matthewdp
- Email: matt@mattpaulson.com

Other Books by Matthew Paulson

40 Rules for Internet Business Success:
Escape the 9 to 5, Do Work You Love
and Build a Profitable Online Business (2014)

Did you know that most "how to make money online" and "passive income" books are written by people that have never actually launched a real online business? Stop reading entrepreneurship books that were written by pretenders. Read *40 Rules for Internet Business Success* and you'll learn from a multi-millionaire entrepreneur that has created multiple six-figure and seven-figure online businesses from scratch.

Matthew Paulson, Founder of MarketBeat.com, has weathered the failures and triumphs of entrepreneurship for more than a decade. *40 Rules for Internet Business Success* is his collection of core principles and strategies he has used to identify new business ideas, launch new companies, and grow his businesses.

By reading *40 Rules for Internet Business Success*, you will learn to:

- Throw away your business plan! Create a scalable business model that actually works.

- Identify a target market that is desperate for your company's products and services.

- Launch your first product or service faster by building a minimum viable business.

- Create a reliable and repeatable marketing strategy to keep new customers coming.

- Understand why most "passive income" business ideas are doomed to fail (and how to beat the odds.)
- Build systems that make your business run like a well-oiled machine.
- Maximize your company's earnings potential with the three keys of revenue growth.

Whether you want to learn how to make money online, create passive income streams or build a massive online business empire, *40 Rules for Internet Business Success* will help you turn your dream of starting a business into reality.

Get Your Copy of *40 Rules for Internet Business Success* **Here:**

http://amzn.to/28Ooy8T

Email Marketing Demystified:

Build a Massive Mailing List, Write Copy that Converts and Generate More Sales (2015)

While many have decried that email is dead, a handful of digital marketers have quietly been using little-known email marketing techniques to generate massive results.

In *Email Marketing Demystified*, digital marketing expert Matthew Paulson reveals the strategies and techniques that top email marketers are currently using to build large mailing lists, write compelling copy that converts and generate millions in revenue using their email lists.

Inside the book, you'll learn how to:

- Build a massive mailing list using 15 different proven list building techniques.
- Write compelling copy that engages your readers and drives them to take action.
- Optimize every step of your email marketing funnel to skyrocket your sales.
- Grow a highly engaged and hungry fan base that will devour your content.
- Create six new revenue streams for your business using email marketing.
- Keep your messages out of the spam folder by following our best practices.

Matthew Paulson has organically grown an email list of more than 400,000 investors and generates more than $2 million per year in revenue using the strategies outlined in *Email Marketing Demystified*. Regardless of what kind of business you are building, email marketing can serve as the rocket fuel that that will skyrocket your business.

Get Your Copy of *Email Marketing Demystified* Here:

http://amzn.to/28XXqpJ

The Ten-Year Turnaround:

Transform Your Personal Finances and
Achieve Financial Freedom in The Next Ten Years (2016)

Do you want to achieve financial freedom, but have no idea how to get there? Do you feel like you just aren't making enough money? Are your personal finances a mess? Are you stuck in debt and wish you could get out? Do you feel like your current financial plan isn't working or isn't working well enough?

If you said yes to any of these questions, it's time for you to begin your Ten-Year Turnaround. *The Ten-Year Turnaround* is a life-changing financial plan that will enable you to turn around your money problems and finally achieve financial freedom.

Here's what you'll learn:

- Grow your income by becoming an expert salary negotiator, starting your own business, or doing a side-hustle on nights and weekends.

- Become an expert money manager and avoid the most common mistakes that prevent people from building wealth.

- Build a dead-simple investment portfolio that will provide a lifetime stream of income.

- Learn proven wealth building techniques that allow anyone to grow their net worth, each and every month.

- Unlock the power of life-long learning and personal networking in your life so that career and business opportunities show up at your door.
- Reduce your taxes, prevent lawsuits, and eliminate financial risk from your life.
- Become a world-class philanthropist and learn how to effectively give money to charity.

In 2004, Matthew Paulson was a broke-and-in-debt college student who earned $7.00 an hour working at McDonalds. By using the personal finance and wealth-building strategies outlined in *The Ten-Year Turnaround*, Matthew was able to build a series of online businesses and amass a personal net worth of more than $10 million by the time he was thirty years old. Whether you're in debt or doing well, you can use the same personal finance strategies Matthew used to build wealth and achieve financial freedom faster than you ever thought possible.

Get Your Copy of *The Ten-Year Turnaround* Here:

http://amzn.to/28QNP4A

Business Growth Day by Day:

*38 Lessons Every Entrepreneur Must Learn
to Get More Done and Make More Money (2016)*

Want to start or grow a business, but aren't getting any traction? Worried that you chose the wrong business idea? Entrepreneurship is a hard game to play, but it doesn't have to be as hard as many people make it out to be. Matthew Paulson outlines the business growth hacking and personal development shortcuts that multi-millionaires use to get ahead of the game in *Business Growth Day by Day*.

Whether you haven't made your first dollar yet or simply can't grow your business to the next level, there's one truth that every entrepreneur must learn:

Working harder isn't the answer.

Putting in enough hours usually isn't the problem. If you are like most entrepreneurs, you are already working harder than anyone else. What's really holding you back from building a successful business? If you're like many entrepreneurs, you're focusing on the wrong parts of your business. You're doing work your team members should be doing. You haven't paid enough attention to critical marketing tasks. You need to fine-tune your business model and pay closer attention to the books. *Business Growth Day by Day* reveals the commonly made, but little-known mistakes that almost every entrepreneur makes, which prevents them from achieving business success.

Here's What You'll Learn:

- The simple strategy that millionaires use to become smarter than everyone else.
- How to recognize and attract new business opportunities (and avoid the wrong ones).
- The single best way to make more money than you are today.
- Why using the word "no" might be the key to unlocking business growth.
- Why SEO, Google AdWords, and Facebook Ads might not be right for your business.
- The biggest small business mistakes commonly made by new entrepreneurs (and how to avoid them).
- How much your business ideas are actually worth—they may be less than you think.
- How your business can maintain an 80% profit margin, each and every month.
- How to effectively pitch your small business and yourself to others.
- When you should quit your day job and go full time with your business.
- What other business books aren't willing to tell you about entrepreneurship.
- Whether you should make a small business plan or just get started launching your business right away.

Matthew Paulson, Founder of MarketBeat.com, USGolfTV, and GoGo Photo Contest, has weathered the failures and triumphs of being an entrepreneur for more than a decade. He has built, grown, and sold multiple six-figure and seven-figure internet businesses using the strategies outlined in this book. Matthew believes that entrepreneurship is the single best way to help others and get what you want out of life. Through his business books, Matthew teaches others to create profitable businesses and achieve financial freedom.

Business Growth Day by Day has been referred to as "one of the must-read small business books to grow your company in 2016 and beyond." *Business Growth Day by Day* is chock-full of unique business ideas, plans, and strategies that will help you take your company to the next level.

Get Your Copy of *Business Growth Day by Day* Here:

http://amzn.to/29JViS7

Simple Savings:

274 Money-Saving Tips That Will Help You Save $1,000 or More Every Month (2016)

Are you tired of having too much month left at the end of your money? Do you feel like there's just never enough money to go around? Would having $100.00, $200.00, or $500.00 extra per month make a big difference in your life? Do you want to save money, but aren't sure where to start? If you can answer yes to any of these questions, *Simple Savings: 274 Money Saving Tips That Will Help You Save $1,000 or More Every Month* is the book for you.

Don't worry! This isn't another one of those books that tell you to pinch pennies and eat nothing but beans and rice. Rather, Simple Savings is chock-full of little-known, but highly effective money-saving strategies that will allow you to live the same lifestyle you are living today while leaving more money in your pocketbook. Authors Matthew Paulson and Toi Williams have collected hundreds of money-saving tips from savvy moms, frugal dads, and other smart shoppers and compiled them into an easy-to-read guide that will teach you to get more value out of each dollar you spend.

By reading *Simple Savings*, you will learn how to:

- Free up room in your budget so that you can spend more money on things that you actually enjoy.
- Reduce your family's grocery budget by $50.00 per week (while buying the same food you are today).

- Dramatically reduce the cost of your cable bill, your cell phone bill, and other nagging, recurring expenses.
- Cut the cost of transportation in half by spending less on gasoline and lowering your vehicle maintenance costs.
- Stop getting ripped off by your bank and get financial services that actually work for you (and not against you).
- Book a first-class trip on an economy budget using little-known travel hacks and other money-saving tips

Want to save money, live better, and spend less?

Saving money has never been easier when you read *Simple Savings: 274 Money Saving Tips That Will Help You Save $1,000 or More Every Month.*

Get your copy of *Simple Savings* and begin living larger on the money you already have.

Get Your Copy of *Simple Savings* Here:

http://www.amztk.com/simplesavings

Automatic Income
How to Use the Power of Dividend Investing to Beat the Market and Generate Passive Income for Life

Disappointed with your current investment portfolio? Do you wish you had more money set aside for retirement? Are you tired of the day-to-day ups and downs of the market? Do you wish there was a strategy that you could follow that actually outperforms the market?

Automatic Income is the best-selling dividend-investing book that teaches investors how to earn double-digit returns using a simple, proven and conservative investment strategy. Written by the founder and editor of MarketBeat, a daily investment newsletter with more than 425,000 subscribers, this invaluable resource will show you how to identify investments that offer lower volatility, higher returns and an automatic income stream of dividends that you can live off of during retirement. This strategy is easy to implement and will set you off on a path toward true financial independence.

Here's what you'll learn:

- How you can create an automatic income stream you can actually live on during retirement.
- How to build an investment portfolio of rock-solid companies that outperform the S&P 500.
- What criteria can identify dividend stocks that consistently return 10% or more per year.
- Which newsletters, websites and other resources you should use to research dividend stocks.
- Why you won't be tempted to cash out your dividend stock portfolio during the next recession.

- How to reduce your tax bill by choosing the right dividend investments and the right accounts.

- Why dividend-growth investing is superior to traditional income investing strategies.

Market risk is near an all-time high and interest rates are at a historic low. There has never been a better time to switch to a more sensible wealth-generation strategy. If you want to improve your market returns, spend less time worrying about money and achieve true financial independence, this book is for you.

Get Your Copy of *Automatic Income* Here:

http://www.automaticincomebook.com